Hiking Colorado:
Eagles Nest Wilderness

By Kim Fenske, JD, MS

Contact: kimlfenske@gmail.com

TABLE OF CONTENTS

NORTHERN EAGLES NEST WILDERNESS

Lower Cataract Lake Loop   4

Elliot Ridge   9

Eaglesmere Lakes   12

Upper Cataract Lake   16

Mirror Lake   21

Tipperary Lake   25

Upper Slate Lake   28

Keller Mountain   32

Upper Boulder Lake   35

SOUTHERN EAGLES NEST WILDERNESS

Willow Lakes   39

South Willow Falls   45

Red Buffalo Pass   48

Lily Pad Lake   52

Eccles Pass   55

Wheeler Lakes   58

WESTERN EAGLES NEST WILDERNESS

Gore Creek   60

Deluge Lake   66

Booth Creek   69

Upper Piney   72

CONTINENTAL DIVIDE

Deer Creek   75

Webster Pass   78

Grays Peak and Torreys Peak   82

Argentine Pass   85

Lenawee Trail   88

TENMILE RANGE

Peak One   92

Wheeler Trail   96

Mohawk Lakes   99

Mayflower Gulch   103

Quandary Peak   106

NORTHERN EAGLES NEST WILDERNESS

Cataract Creek flowing out the eastern side of Lower Cataract Lake

Lower Cataract Lake Loop

Distance: 2 miles

Elevation Profile: 100 feet

Difficulty: Easy

Lower Cataract Lake is one of the favorite destinations for wildflowers in Summit County. More than one hundred species of flowering plant reside in the Montane field, aspen stand, and evergreen forest areas surrounding Cataract Lake. Mule deer, elk, bear, marmot, coyote, Canada goose, and mountain lion are a few of the wildlife species in the vicinity.

The loop around Lower Cataract Lake is two miles, with an elevation gain of a bit more than 100 feet from 8,650 to 8,770 feet in elevation. Although this is one of the easiest hikes in Summit County, give yourself two hours to complete the hike because the beauty of the area will distract you from returning to the parking area.

Proceed through the wooden swing gate or the wooden maze opening in the fence guarding against cattle roaming up from the ranches lower in the valley. Bearing left, follow the wide, rocky path as it dips toward the shore of Lower Cataract Lake. A short distance ahead, you can catch your first view of the lake at a small picnic area.

Continuing clockwise around the lake, cross Cataract Creek on a broad wooden bridge. On the hillside above, fireweed, scarlet gilia, peavine, monument plant, one-sided penstemon, columbine, and wild geranium fill the field. Rounding the lake, the trail enters the Eagles Nest Wilderness Area. Carefully pick a route from among several unmaintained paths through heavy undergrowth on the southern shore. There are small sections of the way that can be boggy and gullied without improved crossings.

Asters, subalpine larkspur, saxifrage, cinquefoil, wild rose, false forget-me-not, groundsel, goldenrod, arrowleaf balsamroot, paintbrush, and harebell line the path. Anise hyssop of the mint family stands in higher wetland areas near cow parsnip and cornhusk lily. Up on drier slopes, stonecrop hides among the sagebrush. The invasive weed oxeye daisy continues to resurge and spread to compete with native plants.

Enter the dense evergreen forest at the southwest corner of the lake and cross Cataract Creek on stepping stones and wooden bridge to view the tumbling waterfalls as the stream enters Lower Cataract Lake. Then, continue north and cross the wetland filled with cornhusk lily, cow parsnip, and asters for an expansive view of the lake from the western shore.

The trail ascends into an aspen grove, climbing onto a bluff on the north shore. From openings in the forest, you can see the Eagles Nest rock formation of Mount Powell, 13,534 feet, looming in the distance above Lower Cataract Lake. Then, the trail descends through an aspen grove and into the lush meadow at the east side of Lower Cataract Lake to complete the loop.

How to Get There

Lower Cataract Lake is 25 miles north of Silverthorne. From the interchange of I-70 and Highway 9 in Silverthorne, drive north for 17 miles to the Mile Marker 118 and turn northwest onto Heeney Road. After passing Mile Marker 5, 22.5 miles from Silverthorne and 5.6 miles from the junction with Highway 9, turn west onto Cataract Creek Road. Travel up a gravel road for 2.4 miles. When you reach a junction past Cataract Creek Campground, proceed straight to reach the Cataract Lake Day Use Area and park south of the locked gate at the end of the road.

Cornhusk lily on the western shore of Lower Cataract Lake

Aspen asters bloom in meadows throughout the wilderness

Fireweed

One-sided Penstemon

Larkspur

Southern end of Elliot Ridge

Elliott Ridge

Distance: 15 miles

Elevation Profile: 1,500 feet

Difficulty: Intermediate

Access to the Eagles Nest Wilderness Area often means hiking uphill for several thousand feet over steep terrain. One exception to the rule of scrambling up steep slopes to reach the tree line is the entry along Spring Creek Ranch Road that leads to Elliott Ridge Trail. Forest Service roads branching near the northern boundary of the Eagles Nest Wilderness Area in Grand County allow access by high clearance vehicles to the heights of the Gore Range.

In the fall, the driving up Spring Creek Ranch Road offers switchbacks overlooking aspen groves in a colorful transition to dormancy. Hunters frequent the elk management area west of the Lower Blue River north of Green Mountain Reservoir because of the meadow breaks created by forest management practices in this area. Forest roads above Spring Creek Ranch Road are also open to Off Highway Vehicle traffic, opening the area to a full range of multiple-use recreation up to the wilderness boundary.

The rugged Gore Range peaks provide a sharp line of delineation between Summit and Eagle Counties. The Elliot Ridge Trail slices the spine of the Gore Range and offers expansive views east to the Ptarmigan Wilderness Area and southwest to the Holy Cross Wilderness Area. Since most of the trail is above the tree line, avoid hiking in the area during thunderstorms.

The hike from the junction at the Blue Lake parking area to Meridian Peak and back is 15 miles in length, with an elevation change from 11,170 feet to 12,630 feet. At an average moving speed of 2 miles an hour, the entire hike takes 8 hours. The drive from Silverthorne is 39 miles to the trailhead, adding another hour to the adventure.

In order to reach the trailhead, drive north from Silverthorne on Highway 9 to Mile Marker 128, passing Williams Peak Road on the right. Turn west on Spring Creek Ranch Road, Grand County 10, and drive up 6 miles to the White River Forest snowmobile winter access parking area. Continue upslope along Forest Service Road 1831, marked with orange diamonds, to reach the Blue Lake junction, 12.7 miles from Highway 9. Beginning at about 11.5 miles, several high-clearance water diversions require cautious driving. The final descent to the Elliott Ridge Trailhead is deeply rutted and may be muddy. Parking along the forest access road above Blue Lake is prudent. As a point of reference, continuing 3 miles down-slope on the next spur of road leads to the Gore Range Trailhead at Mahan Lake.

After passing the little pond on the left referred to as Blue Lake, a registration station marks the trail among a field of boulders. Red elderberry, *Sambucus microbotrys*, marks the entrance to the trail. Then, the trail turns briefly to the west past Sheephorn Mountain and passes patches of Red Prickly Currant, *Grossulariacere Ribes montigenum*. Respect the wilderness beyond the trail signs by leaving no trace of visitation and avoiding much travel off the deeply cut tread onto the patches of surrounding tundra plants above the tree line.

Rising to the ridge, the trail ascends more than a thousand feet over gracefully undulating alpine meadows. Looking eastward, Green Mountain appears directly perpendicular to the trail. After two hours, Mirror Lake Trail crosses a saddle in the ridge, allowing a descent to Mirror, Upper Cataract, Cat, and Surprise lakes. However, another hour of gentle ascent to the South leads to the first summit at 12,400 feet. Continuing along a craggy ridge, on a trail suited to a mountain goat, leads to Meridian Peak at a summit of 12,630 feet. Keep both eyes on the trail immediately ahead and avoid obsessions with the drop-offs on either side of the rocky spine to scramble up to the summit.

From Meridian Peak, observe Lost Lake and Piney Lake about 2,000 feet below to the West in Eagle County. In the East, the Eagles Nest looms beside Mount Powell across a steep basin. Many of the Colorado Fourteeners form the southern horizon. Due to the height of Meridian Peak, the Elliot Ridge Trail provides some of the most dramatic scenery of any hike in Summit County.

How to Get There

Drive north from Silverthorne on Highway 9, passing Green Mountain Reservoir. After entering Grand County, turn left on Spring Creek Ranch Road. Continue ascending west into the forest, passing over water diversions on a rough Forest Service Road. Park near Blue Lake Trailhead.

The Eagles Nest of Mount Powell, 13,534 feet, wilderness namesake

Eaglesmere Lakes

Distance: 7 miles

Elevation Profile: 1,700 feet

Difficulty: Intermediate

Eaglesmere Lakes are found tucked into the Elliott Creek watershed in the Eagles Nest Wilderness Area west of Green Mountain Reservoir. The hike involves five hours of hiking with a little less than two thousand feet of elevation gain, from 8,700 feet to 10,400 feet. The ascent is a typical intermediate hike for Summit County on soft trail, without any mandatory boulder scrambling. Backcountry camping is allowed on the shore, without campfires. Dogs must be leashed in the wilderness area for the protection of wildlife and hikers.

The hike begins in the montane community of a rich variety of wildflowers among aspen groves and sagebrush meadows. More than a hundred species of wildflowers bloom in the vicinity, including monument plant, wild iris, monkshood, wild geranium, larkspur delphinium, and columbine. The small lakes are nestled in a cooler sub-alpine community of dense fir and spruce trees.

For this hike, I carried two liters of ice water, mixed nuts, a fleece, rain jacket, GPS, sunglasses, reading glasses, sunscreen, lip balm, fire starter, two headlamps, pocket knife, cell phone, a few adhesive bandages, camera, and notebook. Mosquito repellent is optional.

I proceeded west through aspen-covered slopes on a moderate and steady ascent, passing many wildflowers and viewing the rugged Eagles Nest ridge on the south side of the Cataract Creek watershed. After 1.8 miles of climbing to about 10,200 feet, two hours from the trailhead, I found a stack of large dead spruce logs marking the junction with the Gore Range Trail.

After stopping to finish my first liter of water, I headed north on the Gore Range Trail for fifteen minutes. At 2.2 miles, I turned west onto the Eaglesmere spur and followed a stream that drained the lower lake.

The gurgling of the stream drowned the noise of my footsteps and, as I rounded a bend, I met a bear approaching me about fifteen steps down the trail. Startled, the bear spun and bounded uphill, rippling its muscular shoulders. The bear's golden fur and powerful shoulder muscles thickened from digging for roots and grubs closely mimicked the form of a grizzly, explaining why there are false sightings in Colorado. This sun-bleached black bear was only slightly bigger than me and quite shy. From my experiences, a grizzly bear will either politely turn and slowly amble off a path or proceed forward, requiring a hiker to step aside.

Bears and other wildlife frequent hiking trails because of the ease of travel compared with beating through brush, picking through boulder fields, and climbing over dead fall trees. Since I also frequent hiking trails and travel quietly, I often bump into bears, elk, mountain goats, ptarmigan, marmots, and other wildlife sharing the paths. I followed the fresh bear tracks through a trace of melting snow to the open space of a campsite on the southern shore of the primary lake.

Hoping to view the tumbling cataracts that fed the lake and get a glimpse of Mount Powell, 13,534 feet, towering over the south side of the valley, I began the slow trek through the forest to circle the lake. Traces of a path dipped into soggy wetlands filled by the early summer snowmelt. Several streams entering the lake at the west end offered a small challenge to finding a dry crossing. At the north end of the lake, I found several campsites with the remains of illegal campfire rings. I also enjoyed magnificent views of Mount Powell reflected in the still water. After an hour of circling the lake, leaping from boulder to boulder across the cataracts of Elliott Creek, I retreated back down toward the trailhead as the sun dipped toward the rim of the Elliott Ridge.

How to Get There

From the interchange of I-70 and Highway 9 in Silverthorne, drive north for 17 miles to the Mile Marker 118 and turn northwest onto Heeney Road. After passing Mile Marker 5, 22.5 miles from Silverthorne, turn west onto Cataract Creek Road. Travel up a gravel road for 2 miles. When you reach a junction, turn right and drive 0.3 miles to reach the Eaglesmere Trailhead Parking Area.

Green gentian monument plant

Globeflower blossoms in spring as soon as snow melts from the wetlands

Marsh marigold shares wetlands with globeflower

Upper Cataract Lake lies north of Mount Powell, 13,543 feet, and the Eagles Nest

Upper Cataract Lake

Distance: 11 miles

Elevation Profile: 2,000 feet

Difficulty: Intermediate

Upper Cataract Lake is located north of Mount Powell, 13,534 feet, below the Eagles Nest for which Eagles Nest Wilderness Area is named. It forms a tributary for the stream of Cataract Creek that flows down a series of steep, rocky cliffs to Lower Cataract Lake. The hike requires about six hours of hiking over 10.5 miles of trail, with an elevation gain of two thousand feet, from 8,600 feet to 10,740 feet.

While the ascent is fairly typical of the steep climbs throughout Summit County, the trail is rough, rocky, and eroded across a couple of miles above the softer trail among the aspen meadows at lower elevations. The distance and elevation gain create a rigorous day hike.

Backcountry camping is available at several lakes in the vicinity, including Surprise Lake, Cat Lake, Tipperary Lake, Upper Cataract Lake, as well as Mirror Lake, located a couple of miles west of Upper Cataract Lake.

Due to heavy use in the wilderness area, no campfires are allowed near the lakes. Dogs are required to be on leash under wilderness recreation regulations throughout Summit County. Mosquitoes are fairly persistent in the boggy areas near the trail, especially annoying during the hot, wet days of early summer.

I froze two liters of water to begin the hike to Upper Cataract Lake, the ice melting along the way to keep me refreshed with cold water throughout the challenging ascent. At Cataract Lake, I used a water filter for refills and easily drank a gallon during the hike. With typical variations in the weather, from hot and sunny to cool rain with hail and lightning, I used layering to remain comfortable during the long day and early evening. I was very thankful to be caught in a brief rainstorm that knocked the mosquitoes out of the air. As usual, I was prepared with a couple of headlamps in the event that my arrival back at the trailhead was delayed. Actually, I arrived at the end of my afternoon hike with a few minutes of alpenglow remaining.

From the Surprise Lake Trailhead, I crossed Cataract Creek and followed the trail that winds south through beautiful wildflower meadows among aspen and spruce trees. My hiking pace dropped as I photographed scarlet gilia, one-sided penstemon, monument plants, blue columbine, wild geranium, purple pea vine, creamy paintbrush, mertensia chiming bells, cow parsnip, and wild iris.

After the first mile and a couple of stream crossings, the forest transforms into standing lodgepole and fallen beetle-killed trees on a steep climb through a hardened clay and rock-strewn gutter up a ridge. The trail levels off and meets the Gore Range Trail at 2.7 miles and 9,900 feet, about two hours into the hike. The next thousand feet of ascent is much more gradual.

Turn right and follow the Gore Range Trail beyond Surprise Lake to the next junction at the start of Upper Cataract Trail. A decade ago, I cut a large dead and down tree that blocked the trail and rolled it down to the junction. This section of tree makes a great resting spot for a snack and water break.

Follow the Upper Cataract Trail west through some boggy sections with drainage gutters on the south side of the trail. Cut sections of logs that formed corrugated bog crossings are now rotted and displaced, so the trail is muddy during the wet season. Beyond the bogs, the trail breaks into an open rock slide that allows the first views of Cat Lake below and Elliott Ridge a few miles farther west. Descending the switchbacks, the trail arrives at Upper Cataract Lake, 5.4 miles and four hours from the trailhead.

Upper Cataract Lake lies directly north of the steep cliffs and rockslide chutes of Mount Powell. The south end of the lake is surrounded by a small table of rock that offers several sites for dispersed camping and gorgeous views of Mount Powell.

How to Get There

From the interchange of I-70 and Highway 9 in Silverthorne, drive north for 17 miles to the Mile Marker 118 and turn northwest onto Heeney Road. After passing Mile Marker 5, 22.5 miles from Silverthorne and 5.6 miles from the junction with Highway 9, turn west onto Cataract Creek Road. Travel up a gravel road for 2.4 miles. When you reach a junction past Cataract Creek Campground, proceed straight to reach the Surprise Lake Trailhead Parking Area on the left side of the road. If you reach the gate at Lower Cataract Lake, you have gone too far.

Blue Columbine blooms along the trail to Upper Cataract Lake

Arnica blooms in early spring in stands of lodgepole pine in the wilderness

Wild iris also emerges from wetlands with early blossoms

Scarlet gilia blooms in open meadows

Purple peavine is a flower of montane fields

Mirror Lake lies east of Elliott Ridge which is visible on the distant horizon

Mirror Lake

Distance: 16 miles

Elevation Profile: 2,400 feet

Difficulty: Intermediate

The north end of the Gore Range provides access to dramatic rock outcroppings, plunging streams filled with prolific trout, and alpine lakes at the base of sheer amphitheaters created by summits exceeding 13,000 feet in height. Winding through the valley of Cataract Creek is the westward ascending Mirror Lake Trail. The 6.5-mile climb to Mirror Lake takes about 5 hours, with Elliott Ridge and Meridian Peak, 12,390 feet, accessible on the trail beyond within another few hours.

The Surprise Lake Trail, begins at 8,597 feet, ascending 2.6 miles to 10,085 feet. Cross the bridge over Cataract Creek, then climb through a sage meadow into the Eagles Nest Wilderness Area. During the first hour of the climb, hike across the rich soil of several aspen meadows filled with blue Colorado columbine, *Aquilegia coerulea*, scarlet fairy trumpet, *Gilia aggregata*, and alpine yarrow, *Achillea alpicola*.

Fleeting distant sightings of bears, coyotes, and mountain lions are common along the lower section of trail near the Cataract Creek. Yellow-bellied marmots dig deep burrows into the rock-strewn sage meadow across from the trailhead. Dogs must be restrained with a leash to protect wildlife and as a courtesy to hikers frequenting the area.

After the meadows and a wide stream crossing, the trail begins a steeper ascent through a dense lodgepole forest. Notice the water diversions made of rock and water checking steps constructed by Forest Service trail crews and Friends of the Eagles Nest Wilderness volunteers. These structures attempt to shed running water from the central tread of the trail and reduce the force of water eroding a deep channel into the mountain slope.

The lower branches of spruce trees and lodgepole pines that interfered with horse and hiker traffic are pruned back to prevent widening of the trail. Trees that fall across the trail are also removed to ease travel and eliminate detour trails that compact soil and destroy the plants in the forest understory.

The Surprise Lake Trail joins the Gore Range Trail near a tumble of downed trees. Turning left, the Gore Range Trail turns east and descends to Otter Creek and passes through private grazing lands along Black Creek. Take the right fork on the Gore Range Trail, heading west, and climb the last 15 minutes to Surprise Lake.

A few large logs form a crossing of the brook that descends from the spongy wetland along the northern shore of Surprise Lake. The woodland along the western shore of the lake is a good example of densely compacted soil, void of plant life from years of heavy use and occupation by campers.

Ascend west for another 30 minutes along the Gore Range Trail to the junction with the Upper Cataract Lake and Mirror Lake Trail. The junction is a great location to drink water and eat lunch before proceeding to the upper lakes.

The next segment of the hike is about 1 hour to Upper Cataract Lake. About mid-way to Upper Cataract Lake is a boggy area lined with many wetland flower blossoms including purple monkshood, *Aconitum columbianum*, mountain goldenrod, *Solidago mutiradiata*, and mountain gentian, *Pneumonaenthe parryi*.

As you break out of the forest overlooking a boulder field, Cat Lake, 10,600 feet, glistens in the afternoon sun a few hundred feet below Upper Cataract Lake. Descend along a winding path across the rock and cross a stream lined with the blooms of white marsh marigold, *Psychrophia leptosepala*, in early summer. Upper Cataract Lake, 10,744 feet, is uphill on the left, with the towering rock formation of the Eagles Nest, 13,397 feet, far above the steep rock face across the lake.

The trail rises to about 11,000 feet, where you can pause to view the Cataract Creek valley and Elliot Ridge from the cliffs at the edge of the trail. Rock switchbacks descend to a crossing of Cataract Creek. Immediately across the creek, observe a confusing labyrinth of social trails descending to the right. In the dark, you can easily miss the stream crossing because of these social trails. If you have any doubts about finding the crossing, throw down the limb of a dead tree to block the descending path and point toward Cataract Creek for the return ascent along the valley wall. Remember to reserve enough energy to ascend to Upper Cataract Lake on the return trip.

Turning southwest, ascend beside the tumbling cataracts that lead almost immediately to the north shoreline of Mirror Lake, 10,560 feet. Proceeding beyond Mirror Lake, you can hike across open wetlands surrounded by an amphitheater formed by Meridian Peak, 12,390 feet, to the west. The Mirror Lake Trail ascends for nearly 2,000 feet to Elliott Ridge, which offers an entire day of adventure in the tundra.

How to Get There

The Mirror Lake Trail is an offshoot of the Surprise Lake Trail at the north end of the Eagles Nest Wilderness Area. Surprise Lake Trailhead is 25 miles north of Silverthorne. Take Highway 9 to the 118-mile marker and turn west on Heeney Road, Summit County Road 30. After 5.3 miles, turn west and climb along Cataract Creek Road, a narrow gravel surface. Pass Cataract Creek Campground on the left side of the road, hidden among the spruce and aspen along the edge of a high desert sage meadow. Immediately past the campground is a junction, with a left fork to the Eaglesmere Trailhead. A few hundred feet ahead is the parking area for Surprise Trailhead.

Rosy paintbrush is prolific on the path to Mirror Lake

The north side of the Cataract Creek is an impenetrable boulder scape

Tipperary Lake lies on a loop between Surprise Lake and Eaglesmere Lakes.

Tipperary Lake

Distance: 9 miles

Elevation Profile: 1,000 feet

Difficulty: Intermediate

The Gore Range Trail extends 43 miles from its southern end at Copper Mountain to Mahan Lake at the northern entrance to the Eagles Nest Wilderness Area. An easy access point, with a loop for day hikers, begins at the Eaglesmere Lakes Trailhead, and ends at Surprise Trailhead, near Lower Cataract Lake. The entire loop takes about six hours for a day hiker, with a starting elevation of 8,700 feet rising to 10,250 feet. For overnight backpackers, dispersed camping solitude is available adjacent to Tipperary Lake, mid-way along the Gore Range Trail loop overlooking Lower Cataract Lake. Backpackers should respect the guidelines for low-impact occupation, at least 100 feet from trail, stream, or lake within the wilderness area.

Proceed up the Eaglesmere Trail along the north side of the valley on a gradual ascent through aspen meadows to reach a junction with the Gore Range Trail. Along the way, the high desert slopes are covered in sage and service berry, then transition to aspen meadows filled in summer with Aspen daisies; *Erigeron speciosa*, fireweed; *Chamerion augustifolium*; and harebell, *Campanula rotundifolia*. Northern bedstraw, *Galium septentrionale*, imported by northern Europeans to fill mattress ticks, hides in the shaded woodland beside brooks that cross the trail. Red columbine, *Aquilegia elegantula*, is among the first of the native wildflowers to cover these slopes among the aspen in spring.

After two and a half hours of uphill climbing, rest on one of the logs at the junction with the Gore Range Trail, at an elevation of about 10,250 feet. Hike south along the Gore Range Trail. The trail crosses a wetland where spotted coralroot, *Corallorhiza maculata*, digests fallen trees and subalpine arnica, *Arnica mollis*, brightens the forest with bright yellow blooms throughout the summer. Within a half-hour, complete the gentle descent along rocky outcroppings covered in stonecrop, *Amerosedum lanceolatum*, to reach the tumbling flow of Cataract Creek. Cast a line in the deep pools to enjoy the tug of a stunted trout anxious to snap at any morsel dropped into these waters or continue along the trail for another half-hour to a short spur down to Tipperary Lake.

From Tipperary Lake, the Gore Range Trail rises within a forty-five-minute hike to a junction with the Upper Cataract Trail, where a large cross-cut carved log marks another great spot for a rest and snack. Continue east for a half-hour to Surprise Lake, taking a sharp left turn at the next junction to leave the Gore Range Trail. The final steep descent through lodgepole pines and several meadows to Surprise Trailhead takes a little more than an hour.

How to Get There

Eaglesmere Lakes Trailhead is approximately 24 miles north of Silverthorne. Take Highway 9 north to the 118-mile marker, then turn left onto Heeney Road and drive four miles along the west side of the Blue River and Green Mountain Reservoir. Turn left again at Cataract Creek Road, drive 2 miles up the gravel road to Cataract Creek Campground. Immediately past the campground, the road splits. Vehicle parking to the left is Surprise Trailhead, while the parking loop at the end of the right branch of the road is for Eaglesmere Trailhead.

A mule deer buck stands alert near Eaglesmere Lakes

Upper Slate Lake offers a calming reflection in the evening light

Upper Slate Lake

Distance: 24 miles

Elevation Profile: 2,000 feet

Difficulty: Advanced

As I descended from Upper Slate Lake through rabbitbrush and sage, I whistled, "It's a long way to Tipperary," after hiking a couple hours in the darkness. In answer to my tune, a wolf howled across the valley from the ridge behind me. Only the single, low, long howl created an echo against the opposing slope on the south side of Slate Creek. The sound of the wolf provided me with comfort, knowing the wolf shared with me the desire to roam a great distance to explore remote and solitary places

My long day hike began at the Rock Creek Trailhead at about 9,500 feet a half-mile east of the Gore Range Trail. This late-summer hike, I decided to travel light and fast with scattered showers in the forecast. When I reached the Gore Range Trail about noon, I turned north and ascended the ridge at the eastern base of Keller Mountain. I descended on the switchbacks into the next watershed, arriving at the bridge across Boulder Creek an hour later. Despite the light mist created by passing clouds, I appreciated the cool temperature and lack of mosquitoes.

An hour and a half later, I reached the watershed of Harrigan Creek after climbing over a second ridge, 3.7 miles from the trailhead. I scooped a liter of water into my filter and filled my water bottle at the double-plank bridge across the trickling stream.

I quickened my pace over the gentle slope into the next watershed, passing through a mixed forest of spruce, fir, aspen, and willows in the boggy lowlands before Slate Creek. As I descended on switchbacks, I found dark blue scat in the trail, evidence of the black bears grazing on ripe blueberries along the way. After three hours, 6 miles from the trailhead at about 9,050 feet, I arrived at the fallen pine tree that served as the substitute bridge to cross over to the north side of Slate Creek.

Slate Creek tumbles to the valley below the lakes

The abundant clumps of blue columbine, scarlet gilia, mariposa lily, false forget-me-not, asters, wild geranium, monkshood, peavine, and paintbrush of early summer were gone from the meadow before the intersection of the Gore Range Trail and the Slate Creek Trail. I turned west, crossing the dry field of rabbitbrush, cinquefoil, and sage for a few miles before entering the dense fir forest and willow wetlands on the steep slope beside tumbling cataracts falling down steep, rocky steps below Slate Lake. The heavy growth intruding on the thin, lightly-treaded trail held enough raindrops from the dissipated showers to keep my quick-drying trail slacks damp.

After 10 miles of hiking, I saw the shore of Slate Lake, a thousand feet above the Gore Range Trail. I crossed a log jam and scrambled over the rock pads on the shoreline to enjoy the reflections of the rugged ridgeline high above the fir trees, willow tangles, and cattails that surrounded the lake.

During the next hour-and-a-half, I ascended the next two miles up the steep trail that winds past stacked boulders and meanders through a final willow bog before a short descent into the bowl that contains Upper Slate Lake at 10,876 feet. I arrived as the last rays of sunlight provided an alpenglow across the cliffs. The summit of the 13,000-foot peaks separate the Slate Creek watershed from the Piney River Valley immediately west of this amphitheater.

In the evening light, I enjoyed the reflective pool of Upper Slate Lake, then began the twelve-mile trek back to the trailhead at Rock Creek. I relied entirely on the warm glow of my headlamp during my return hike through the new moon night. The familiar trail passed easily beneath my feet, although the return hike requires a climb out of the three watersheds to reach the trailhead. An hour past midnight, I left the Gore Range Trail and began the final descent into the Blue River Valley.

How to Get There

Upper Slate Lake and Slate Lake are accessible from the Rock Creek Trailhead. From Silverthorne, drive north on Highway 9 to the 109 Mile Marker at Blue River National Forest Campground. Turn left and ascend west on the gravel road for 1.2 miles, then turn left onto Forest Service 1350. The road terminates at the Rock Creek Trailhead parking area.

Lower Slate Lake offers a beautiful setting for dispersed camping

A male ptarmigan, identified by the orange over his eye, forages in the tundra

Keller Mountain has a long ridge that requires a scramble west to the summit

Keller Mountain

Distance: 12 miles

Elevation Profile: 4,000 feet

Difficulty: Advanced

Keller Mountain, 13,085 feet, in the North Rock Creek watershed, offers an opportunity to explore an historic mining area and observe waves of brilliantly-colored aspen groves during the fall season. Hikers are enveloped by the ragged ridges of the southern Gore Range that can be viewed from beyond tree-line by ascending Keller Mountain to a boulder-strewn ridge.

Although I completed a rigorous day hike of 12 miles and 4,000 vertical feet, a casual hiker can shorten this to an easy 5-mile round-trip stroll from the upper Rock Creek Trailhead parking area with a vertical ascent of only 1,000 feet to the Boss Mine ruins. The Boss Mine area is obvious due to the large, barren yellow sulfide tailings piles that cover a large swath on the south face of Keller Mountain.

The Boss Mine produced around $200,000 worth of high-grade Argentite silver ore from 1882 to 1897 from veins less than five feet wide. Gold, lead, zinc, and copper were also present in the extracted ores. Acidic run-off containing toxic heavy metals will persist for centuries from the abandoned mines throughout Colorado.

After bottoming-out on many potholes and exposed rocks a few weeks earlier, I decided to park at the lower Rock Creek parking area, 1.5 miles below the Rock Creek Trailhead. In the past, I have paid towing fees to get my own all-wheel-drive vehicle and a Good Samaritan's pick-up truck down off this Forest Service Road after an early snowstorm coated the surface in slippery powder. As I walked along the road admiring the gurgling creek among willow thickets and aspens, I realized that a grader had recently leveled many of the hazards that had punished my vehicle during the previous month.

From the Rock Creek Trailhead, I proceeded west into the Eagles Nest Wilderness Area and continued straight at the intersection with the Gore Range Trail. After two hours, I reached the Boss Mine, four miles from the lower parking area at 10,280 feet. I ascended a couple of quick switchbacks and continued west on the trail that leaves the mine tailings behind and enters avalanche chutes covered in densely-packed aspen saplings. One-third of a mile beyond the Boss Mine, at 10,400 feet, I found an open meadow on a steep slope and chose a path for my scramble to the ridge of Keller Mountain.

Two hours later, I reached the exposed ridge at an elevation of 11,850 feet, 5.5 miles from my start. I continued through the boulder field that rose above the krummholz and tundra turf toward the summit. Another hour passed as I ascended the next thousand feet, scrambling ahead on the sharp spine of rock that forms the western end of Keller Mountain.

I captured photographs of the Boulder Creek watershed that lies north of Keller Mountain, as well as the ridge of Willow Mountain that peeked over the southern wall of North Rock Creek Valley. The surrounding peaks own obscure titles, including Peak X, Peak Z, Mount Solitude, North Traverse Peak, and Climber's Point.

I began my descent, stumbling on a male ptarmigan that was foraging for wildflower seeds in the boulder field at 12,500 feet. The distinctive blaze orange stripe over his eye identified his sex. I observed his dining activity for a while, the bird blending well with the rocks, despite the transition of his plumage from the mottled brown of summer to the all-white feathers of winter.

I quickly cut a path east on unknown terrain, being careful to avoid falling from small rock outcrops. I descended through steep slopes swept clean by frequent snow slides and wandered past the ruins of several mining cabins before connecting with the main trail that passed out of the valley. As the sun sank below the ridge of the Gore Range nine hours after my start, I arrived at the lower parking area.

How to Get There

Drive north from Silverthorne to the 109 Mile Marker and turn west on Rock Creek Road. Continue up the road for 1.5 miles to the low-clearance and winter parking area. If you have a vehicle with reasonably high clearance to pass over water diversions, potholes, and small stones, turn left onto the Forest Service Road and continue another 1.5 miles to the Rock Creek Trailhead parking area. Along the way, the rocky road passes aspen groves, dispersed campsites, and the gurgling, willow-lined shores of North Rock Creek. Take the Rock Creek Trail west to the junction with the Gore Range Trail and continue straight up the North Rock Creek Valley.

Keller Mountain provides views of the Blue River Valley and Ptarmigan Wilderness

Upper Boulder Lake in late June provides a challenging and beautiful destination

Upper Boulder Lake

Distance: 12 miles

Elevation Profile: 1,500 feet

Difficulty: Advanced

The Eagles Nest Wilderness Area is 133,496-acres of forest lands protected in a primitive condition by Congress in 1976. The wilderness area was carved out of undeveloped and abandoned parts of the Gore Mountain Range. The Gore Range was named after Sir George Gore who hired Jim Bridger to guide him on a hunting expedition in 1854. Gore took 30 wagons and 50 servants on a 6,000-mile expedition through the Rocky Mountains, killing thousands of big game animals and discovering gold near Piney Lake north of Vail.

This initiated a period more than fifty years in length of panning placer and refining low-grade ores. Throughout the region, low-grade silver ores were pulverized at stamping mills. Then, silver was extracted by amalgamation using mercury and copper sulfate. After bonding and isolating the silver with mercury, the mercury was vaporized at the expense of mercury equal to or greater than the weight of silver obtained. The resulting contamination of refining locations as well as leaching of toxic minerals from shaft mines has damaged the quality of many Colorado waterways for more than a century.

One of the shaft mines in the Eagles Nest Wilderness Area is the Boss Mine at the southern base of Keller Mountain, 13,085 feet, at western end of the Rock Creek Trail. The Boss Mine extracted primarily silver ore from 6,000 feet of tunnels dug through narrow veins of ore averaging three feet in width. The recovered ore was refined into $220,000-worth of silver during the period from 1882 to 1897.

Boulder Lake and Upper Boulder Lake are popular hiking destinations located on the opposite side of Keller Mountain from the Boss Mine in the Boulder Creek watershed. Boulder Lake is 3 miles north of the Rock Creek Trailhead at 9,750 feet. Upper Boulder Lake is a difficult ascent to 11,000 feet, 3 miles beyond Lower Boulder Lake.

From the Rock Creek Trailhead at 9,500 feet, hike west on the Rock Creek Trail for a half-mile to the junction with the Gore Range Trail. Turn right and hike north along the Gore Range Trail, passing wetlands filled with cornhusk lily, cow parsnip, chiming bells, monkshood, false forget-me-not, paintbrush, and arnica. After hiking 2 miles, about one hour, to the ridge of Keller Mountain at 10,100 feet, several large boulders offer seating to rest at the highest point on the trek to Lower Boulder Lake.

Descend from the ridge on a half-mile of switchbacks and cross the bridge over Boulder Creek. The Boulder Creek Trail extends west from a junction immediately across the bridge. However, continue north on the Gore Range Trail and take the next trail west to reach the north shore of Lower Boulder Lake.

Lower Boulder Lake is a glistening reflection pool with the crest of Keller Mountain dominating the background. The trail continues west on the north side of the lake, passing a wetland area essential for nurturing moose and elk roaming the area. For an overnight hike, several established dispersed camping sites exist near the shore of Boulder Creek for the next mile of gradual ascent to 10,200 feet.

The trail from Lower Boulder Lake to Upper Boulder Lake is much more challenging and dangerous. A meadow opens the forest at 10,200 feet with a log crossing. The trail crosses Boulder Creek to the south side and proceeds west beside the stream.

My notes from a decade ago bear a strong resemblance to a recent ascent, mentioning many dead and down logs across the trail. The trail vanishes or becomes confusing with several social trails branching off, equally tempting directions to attack the physical barriers ahead. The pace grinds to less than a mile of progress an hour caused by pathfinding and scrambling up several cliffs. Since no certain and easy trail can be constructed through this steep and narrow watershed, the Forest Service does not maintain a path to Upper Boulder Lake and discourages visitors by not circulating a Recreational Opportunity Guide to the area. Undertake the climb to Upper Boulder Lake at your own risk and potential reward.

How to Get There

Drive north 8 miles from the Silverthorne interchange with I-70 to the 109 Mile Marker on Highway 9 North. Turn west on Rock Creek Road, across from the Forest Service Blue River Campground. After ascending 1.2 miles, turn left at the winter parking area. The Forest Service Road 1350 is reasonably maintained to allow low-clearance vehicles to continue 1.5 miles to the Rock Creek Trailhead. Along the way, there are dispersed camping areas among aspen and lodgepole pine trees and the gurgling, willow-lined shores of North Rock Creek.

Dispersed camping rules advise that campsites must be 100 feet from waterway, trail, or road. However, some established non-conforming campsites exist. Dispersed campers in the Eagles Nest Wilderness Area should always minimize impact by packing out all trash, avoiding lakeside campsites, and not building campfires. Dogs must be kept on leash for the safety of wildlife, other hikers, and pets. All motorized and wheeled activities are prohibited in wilderness areas. Heavy use of the wilderness has degraded the appearance of areas, permanently compacted soils, sterilized soils with campfires, and stripped areas of fuel wood. User abuse encourages policy makers to tighten regulations, require backcountry permits, and close access to damaged areas.

A cow moose watches over her calf near the shore of Lower Boulder Lake

Lower Boulder Lake in the calm of a summer evening

SOUTHERN EAGLES NEST WILDERNESS

Middle Willow Lake is surrounded by a ragged amphitheater and fir trees

Willow Lakes

Distance: 13 miles

Elevation Profile: 2,400 feet

Difficulty: Intermediate

The Willow Lakes of the Gore Range are one of my favorite day hike destinations in the State of Colorado. The lakes are nestled in the North Willow Creek watershed, surrounded by the sharp, ragged ridge of Red Peak, 13,189 feet, to the south and Willow Peak, 13,333 feet, forming the wall of the bowl to the north.

The hike is a bit beyond intermediate with an elevation gain of 2,400 feet, from 9,000 to 11,400 feet, and a strenuous distance of 13 miles to 18 miles, depending on which access route is taken. The effort is well-rewarded with an abundance of wildflowers and several alpine pools set against a dramatic rock wall backdrop. Give yourself 8 hours of daylight to enjoy the hike.

On a cool morning, I set out from the Willowbrook Trailhead parking area. I carried two liters of ice water, a few ounces of nuts, pound of fruit, rain jacket, fleece, and the usual emergency gear. In my daypack and pockets, I always carry two headlamps, a means to start a fire, pocketknife, cell phone, bandages, and tissues.

Despite being a weekday, the parking area was nearly full. However, I quickly realized that all of the other hikers were headed west on the short hike to South Willow Falls, while I was turning north on the Ditches Trail. As I ascended a few hundred feet over the next half-mile, I encountered white yarrow, blue false forget-me-not, purple aster, wild geranium, rose bush, midnight blue monkshood, mariposa lily, arnica, and senecio in the damp, fertile montane meadows.

At the junction with the North Willow Creek Trail, I turned left for a steeper climb west to merge with the Three Peaks Trail, a mile from the trailhead at 9,525 feet. I made a mental note to bear right and head south at this junction on my return. A few tenths of a mile later, I headed north on the east bank of North Willow Creek.

An hour after beginning the hike, I entered the quarter-mile span of blown-down lodgepole pine trees that a volunteer crew with the Friends of the Eagles Nest Wilderness Area and Forest Service sawyers cleared several years ago. The sacrifice of this patch of wilderness pines to a wind storm opened the forest floor to light, allowing a profusion of paintbrush and other wildflowers to fill the void.

At 2.8 miles, I completed my first 1,200 feet of ascent, half of the vertical component of the hike in about an hour and a half. I sat down at the junction of the Gore Range Trail with the Willow Lakes Trail and satiated my hunger and thirst on a fallen log.

Climbing west on a steep ridge, I met the Salmon Lake Trail at an elevation of 11,100 feet, after hiking 4.5 miles. As I continued southwest on the Willow Lakes Trail, the path leveled-off. Within the next mile, I met three retreating day hikers who were heading south to Buffalo Mountain and two overnight backpackers who were returning to the Rock Creek Trailhead. Within a mile, I arrived in the solitude of Lower Willow

Lake, a small pond with the typical shape of an alpine lake trapped behind a landslide of boulders from the opposing walls of Red Peak and Willow Peak.

Four hours into the ascent, I reached Middle Willow Lake, 6.0 miles from the trailhead at 11,333 feet. On the northern shore, I found rosy paintbrush, chiming bells, kings crown, snowball saxifrage, purple fringe, dark beardtongue, and elephant tusk. I also found mosquitoes, rumbling thunder over Red Peak, and rain clouds closing the bluebird sky.

I hurried along to Upper Willow Lake, 6.5 miles from the trailhead at 11,380 feet, arriving four and a half hours after my departure. After briefly pausing to enjoy views of the lake and watching a marmot scurrying among the boulders, I retreated and arrived back at the trailhead three hours later.

Mountain gentian blooms on high slopes among the tundra grasses

Upper Willow Lake lies at tree-line, surrounded by a carpet of green turf

How to Get There

Day hikers can save a few miles of hiking compared to other approaches by heading north on Highway 9 in Silverthorne for 2 miles. Turn left into the Willowbrook subdivision and drive 1 mile west to the daytime parking area at the Willowbrook Trailhead. Then, take the Ditches Trail north for 0.6 miles before heading west into the Eagles Nest Wilderness Area. A Summit Stage public transit bus can also drop you at the base of the Willowbrook subdivision at the top of each hour.

On an overnight backpacking trip, one way to reach Willow Lakes is from the Buffalo Cabin Trail at the top of Ryan Gulch Road. From the junction of the I-70 and Highway 9 in Silverthorne, drive north for 0.3 miles and turn left on Wildernest Road. Go 0.5 miles before turning left onto Ryan Gulch Road. Drive up the base of Buffalo Mountain for 3.7 miles and stop at the Buffalo Cabin Trailhead, parking on the left side of the road. Take the trail northwest around the base of Buffalo Mountain to the junction with the Gore Range Trail. Proceed east, then north on the Gore Range Trail to the Salmon Willow Trail and ascend southwest.

Another overnight approach is to drive north from Silverthorne to the 109 Mile Marker and turn west on Rock Creek Road. Continue up the road for 1.5 miles and turn left onto the Forest Service Road and go another 1.5 miles to the Rock Creek Trailhead parking. Take the Rock Creek Trail to the junction with the Gore Range Trail. Then, you will head south, crossing North Rock Creek and South Rock Creek, before turning southwest on the Salmon Willow Trail.

Mariposa lily blooms in open meadows

Monkshood blooms in wetlands

Elephant tusk resembles its title

South Willow Creek watershed looking east above South Willow Falls

South Willow Falls

Distance: 4 miles

Elevation Profile: 500 feet

Difficulty: Intermediate

South Willow Falls is located in the valley between the steep, rocky slopes of Red Peak, 13,189 feet, and Buffalo Mountain, 12,777 feet. The pass itself is part of ridge over the amphitheater bowl that lies west of Buffalo Mountain. South Willow Creek forms from the tributary brooks pouring out of the great bowl of dense evergreen forest west of Buffalo Mountain.

The hike is intermediate in grade, rising and descending a few hundred feet as it follows the base of Buffalo Mountain for 1.5 miles. South Willow Falls is 2 miles from the Buffalo Cabin Trailhead, with about 500 feet of elevation for a profile, an easy day hike by mountain standards.

Where there are breaks in the tangle of firs and spruce trees, many delicate wetland wildflowers and ferns grow. White bog orchid, king's crown, red elephant tusk, blue columbine, dark purple monkshood also known as the poisonous wolf bane used by assassins in medieval times, and blue mountain chimes or *mertensia* bloom during the mid-summer.

Carry at least one liter of cold water on this 4-mile hike. Plan to be on the trail for at least two hours. Pack a fleece and rain jacket to be ready for afternoon thunderstorms that are very common during the summer. Prepare yourself for a few hundred feet of climbing out of the valley to return to Buffalo Cabin Trailhead, including a snack for extra energy.

Beginning at the Buffalo Cabin Trailhead, 9,850 feet, hike northwest for a half-mile to a junction where the trail turns left for the ascent to the summit of Buffalo Mountain. At the junction, proceed straight and descend a few hundred feet over the next half-mile. The trail crosses a small boulder field and proceeds on the dike holding back the water in a small diversion ditch. After a few hundred steps, the trail continues on an abrupt descent to the right and crosses several streams of South Willow Creek through a broad wetland.

Follow the gravel beds contained between logs to follow the trail to the north side of South Willow Creek. The trail meets a junction with the Gore Range Trail at 1.5 miles, 9,500 feet. From the junction, South Willow Falls is only a half-hour climb. Beyond the falls, several more tumbling cataracts of South Willow Creek drop through the steep valley from the west and invite further exploration. From the rock outcroppings on the trail, the scenic view east of the valley includes the Williams Fork Range, part of the Ptarmigan Wilderness Area.

How to Get There

From the junction of the I-70 and Highway 9 in Silverthorne, drive north for 0.3 miles and turn left on Wildernest Road. Go 0.5 miles before turning left onto Ryan Gulch Road. Drive up the base of Buffalo Mountain for 3.7 miles to Buffalo Cabin Trailhead, parking on the left side of the road.

South Willow Falls between Buffalo Mountain and Red Peak

Red Buffalo Pass leads west to Gore Creek, descending into Vail

Red Buffalo Pass

Distance: 10 miles

Elevation Profile: 2,500 feet

Difficulty: Intermediate

Red Buffalo Pass is located west of Silverthorne and east of Vail. The pass is named for the surrounding mountains of Red Peak, 13,189 feet, and Buffalo Mountain 12,777. The pass itself is part of ridge over the amphitheater bowl that lies west of Buffalo Mountain. Buffalo Pass, 11,770 feet, is the ridge of the Gore Range that forms South Willow Creek watershed to the east and Gore Creek to the west.

The hike is intermediate in grade and strenuous due to the five-mile distance from the Buffalo Cabin Trailhead to Red Buffalo Pass, with 2,000 feet of vertical gain. The lower, dense evergreen forest provides opportunities to view wildflowers including arnica, paintbrush, mountain chimes, and columbine. The upper tundra meadows fill with avalanche lilies as soon as the snow fields melt in early summer. In the wetlands, globeflower and marsh marigolds line alpine brooks. The most outstanding scenery is found viewing the back slopes of Buffalo Mountain and sharp ridge of Eccles Pass to the south.

Beginning at the Buffalo Cabin Trailhead, 9,850 feet, hike northwest for a half-mile to a junction where the trail turns left for the ascent to the summit of Buffalo Mountain. At the junction, proceed straight and descend a few hundred feet over the next half-mile. The trail follows an old water diversion ditch, subsequently dropping to the right to cross the several streams of South Willow Creek. While the Friends of the Eagles Nest Wilderness Area worked with the Forest Service packing gravel into an intact walkway through the wetlands, several bridges across the streams are broken. In high water, crossing requires nimble path-finding skills. Continuing north, the trail meets a junction with the Gore Range Trail at 1.5 miles, 9,500 feet.

Uneva Pass leads into the Meadow Creek watershed that descends into Frisco

Turn left, climbing on switchbacks through the dense forest beside many tumbling cataracts of South Willow Creek. Begin the ascent of 2,000 feet over the next three miles to reach the treeless heights of Red Buffalo Pass. Along the way, enjoy magnificent cliffs and avalanche chutes on both Red Peak and Buffalo Mountain. Step across several snow-fed streams that you can tap for cool, refreshing water. Enjoy the lush wetland wildflowers growing in the rock-strewn meadows below the peaks.

From Red Buffalo Pass, enjoy views of the Ptarmigan Wilderness Area that lies in the Williams Fork Range in the east, across the Blue River Valley and beyond Silverthorne. The South Willow Creek watershed is a carpet of dense fir and spruce forest spread below Buffalo Mountain. Eccles Pass provides the Gore Range Trail with access to Meadow Creek, North Ten Mile Creek, Officers Gulch, and Wheeler Lakes near Copper Mountain. To the west, the Gore Creek Trail descends into Vail.

How to Get There

From the junction of the I-70 and Highway 9 in Silverthorne, drive north for 0.3 miles and turn left on Wildernest Road. Go 0.5 miles before turning left onto Ryan Gulch Road. Drive up the base of Buffalo Mountain for 3.7 miles and stop at the Buffalo Cabin Trailhead, parking on the left side of the road.

The western slope of Buffalo Mountain from the base of Red Buffalo Pass

Avalanche lilies carpet the upper watershed of South Willow Creek in spring

Lily Pad Lake with Peak One in the distance

Lily Pad Lake

Distance: 2 miles

Elevation Profile: 200 feet

Difficulty: Beginner

Nestled among a dense lodgepole pine forest at the southeast edge of the Eagles Nest Wilderness Area, the Lily Pad Lake Trail offers easy access to great views of the Blue River Valley surrounding Dillon Reservoir. Lily Pad Lake Trail is a welcome path for a family trek in hiking boots, snowshoes, or cross-country skis. No mountain biking is permitted and pets should be leashed beyond the wilderness boundary.

The trailhead begins on the eastern face of Buffalo Mountain in the Wildernest development, a few miles above Silverthorne. In order to reach the trailhead area by public transit, hop on a Wildernest Summit Stage from the bus transfer station near the Silverthorne Post Office, west of Highway 9 north at Third Street.

By personal vehicle, take the Silverthorne exit from I-70 and turn left at the first intersection on Highway 9 north of the freeway. Begin traveling west along Wildernest Road, the frontage access wrapped around the base of Buffalo Mountain. Follow the switchbacks by turning right onto Ryan Gulch Road. Proceed 3.6 miles to the shared parking pad for the Buffalo Mountain Trail and Lily Pad Lake Trail.

The lower trailhead is the entry to the Buffalo Mountain Trail that climbs 3,000 feet to the northwest to reach the summit of Buffalo Mountain. Farther up the road is the gated Forest Service Road that serves as the trailhead for the Lily Pad Lake Trail.

The Lily Pad Lake Trail, at 9,830 feet, follows the topography to the south. About forty minutes, the Lily Pad Lake Trail meets the Salt Lick Trail, at 10,000 feet, where the trail turns to the right and follows a water diversion ditch. The trail continues through a wetland area where moose are frequently sighted. In a bit over an hour, the trail reaches fraternal twin ponds, Upper Lily Pad Lake and Lower Lily Pad Lake, before descending to the Meadow Creek Trailhead near Frisco.

Upper Lily Pad Lake is a shallow pond covered in yellow water lilies in summer and frequented by ducks. Across a small earthen berm, Lower Lily Pad Lake, provides a view of the north end of the Ten Mile Range above the lodgepole forest. To the north, the summit of Buffalo Mountain rises above the shoreline.

Beyond the beaver dam that helps close the outlet to the lake, the trail drops through open meadows and aspen glens filled with wildflowers in summer. After a snack near the lakes, the trek back along the same trail returns to the parking area. An alternative adventure continues south to the junction with the Meadow Creek Trail and descends into Frisco. A short walk along a gravel frontage road leads across the freeway overpass to the Summit Stage transfer center in Frisco, where a free bus to Silverthorne can be found.

Calypso orchids bloom in wetland areas in early summer

Eccles Pass lies north of Meadow Creek, across from this beaver pond

Eccles Pass

Distance: 15 miles

Elevation Profile: 2,700 feet

Difficulty: Intermediate

The hiking trails forming a loop around Buffalo Mountain, 12,777 feet, stretch across 15 miles. Starting at the Meadow Creek Trailhead, the trail climbs west to meet the Gore Range Trail at the base of Eccles Pass. The trail ascends 2,700 vertical feet from 9,170 feet to 11,900 feet at Eccles Pass. From Eccles Pass, the Gore Range Trail drops into the watershed of South Willow Creek, immediately south of Red Peak, 13,189 feet. The Gore Range Trail passes South Willow Falls, then meets a connecting trail from South Willow Creek to the Buffalo Cabin Trailhead. Across Ryan Gulch Road, the Lily Pad Lakes Trail forms the final link, heading south to return to the Meadow Creek Trailhead.

On the first day of summer, the snowpack is quickly trickling into Meadow Creek to reveal mountain wildflowers popping up from the forest duff. The first section of the Meadow Creek Trail rises through aspen meadows 0.7 miles to the junction with the Lily Pad Trail at 9,610 feet. Below the dense aspen leaves, purple lupine; pea vine; white wild geranium; and red columbine are bursting from the ground. The forest abruptly transitions to dry lodgepole pine forest where yellow arnica blooms in the shade near bundles of hollygrape and spears of paintbrush.

At 10,000 feet, the trail crosses Meadow Creek and continues to climb on the north side of the stream for the next mile. The forest begins a transition to fir and spruce, retaining several feet of snowdrifts below the boughs. As the forest opens into damp meadows, marsh marigold and globeflower line the rivulets gathering the snowmelt. The trail reaches the next crossing of Meadow Creek, 3 miles from the trailhead at 10,970 feet.

After another mile, a thick snowfield forms a snow bridge that crosses Meadow Creek. On the north side of the stream, the Meadow Creek Trail terminates at a junction with the Gore Range Trail. More than 5 miles and four hours from the start of the hike, the Gore Range Trail ascends on switchbacks through deep patches of snow to reach the saddle of Eccles Pass at 11,900 feet.

From Eccles Pass, the Ten Mile Range stretches across the horizon south of the Meadow Creek watershed. North of the pass, the saddle of Red Buffalo Pass marks the origin of the Gore Creek Trail that follows the flow of snowmelt west to Vail. Across the bowl draining east into South Willow Creek, the ragged ridge of Red Peak towers over boulder fields raked raw by avalanches.

Nearly two miles of the Gore Range Trail are covered by rippling snowfield. By crossing the valley and searching among the boulders at the base of red peak, the trail may reveal itself on the north side of South Willow Creek below 11,000 feet.

The trail descends to the cliffs at South Willow Falls, 10 miles from the trailhead at 10,000 feet. A half-mile below the falls, there is a junction of the Gore Creek Trail and a feeder trail that crosses South Willow Creek and wraps around the east face of Buffalo Mountain to reach the Buffalo Cabin Trailhead. The log bridges are rotten and broken, so be prepared to engage in a bit of path-finding to cross South Willow Creek and proceed up a few hundred vertical feet for two miles on a neglected trail.

From the Buffalo Cabin Trailhead, continue south on Lily Pad Lakes Trail for 2 miles. The Lily Pad Lakes Trail passes through huge open areas created from fallen lodgepole pine trees that were killed by infestation of the mountain pine beetle. Even in the night, Lily Pad Lakes Trail is easy to follow. Progress of the trek can be monitored by the movement of Silverthorne street lights, the beacon of the lodge at the summit of Keystone, and the lights of Frisco on the edge of Dillon Reservoir.

Passing between the two ponds of Lily Pad Lakes, 14 miles from the beginning of the loop, the trail descends a few hundred feet through aspen groves to a substantial bridge across the cataracts of Meadow Creek and meets the Meadow Creek Trail. The final link drops 400 feet back to the Meadow Creek Trailhead, retracing the first steps of the day.

How to Get There

Meadow Creek Trailhead is one-half mile southwest of the round-about on the exit from I-70 at Mile Marker 203, off Summit Boulevard and Highway 9 in Frisco. The trailhead parking area is at the end of the gravel frontage road across the freeway and north of the Frisco Transit Center. Other access points to the loop around Buffalo Mountain include the Buffalo Cabin Trailhead at the top of Ryan Gulch Road in Wildernest and the Willowbrook Trailhead a mile from the entrance to Willowbrook in Silverthorne. The Summit Stage public transit routes provide access to these three trailheads.

Red Buffalo Pass provides passage west to Gore Creek from South Willow Creek

Wheeler Lakes, near tree-line, can be frozen though June

Wheeler Lakes

Distance: 6 miles

Elevation Profile: 1,600 feet

Difficulty: Intermediate

The trail to Wheeler Lakes begins on the Gore Range Trail north of Copper Mountain. After hiking across the freeway overpass, enter the Gore Range Trail on the west side of the road. Continue across an open meadow until the trail turns up a steep ravine. An hour above the freeway, the trail crosses a stream at the boundary of the Eagles Nest Wilderness Area. A downed log at the wilderness boundary, elevation around 10,200 feet, provides a good resting spot.

Continue north for another hour and bear right on the Wheeler Lakes Trail. The trail to the north proceeds across a wetland area to Wheeler

Lakes within a half-hour, rising to a ridgeline at 11,200 feet that provides a view northeast over Officers Gulch.

From the junction in the trails west of Wheeler Lakes, the Gore Range Trail levels off and continues north for more than forty miles to Grand County. An hour farther along the Gore Range Trail, a two-hour descent may be made along the north side of the main stream channel to reach Officers Gulch Pond, 3 miles northeast of Copper Mountain. From the pond, continue under the freeway, cross Tenmile Creek, and hike up the Recreation Path to Copper Mountain.

How to Get There

Copper Mountain is fortunate to be located immediately south of the Eagles Nest Wilderness Area. Many miles of remote snowshoe and cross-country ski experience is accessible along the Gore Range Trail, with the trail to Wheeler Lakes beginning across the freeway from Copper Mountain Village. The official entry registration site is along the wetlands located a half-mile east of Copper Mountain at the scenic area turn-out. Visitors to Copper Mountain can park at the trailhead parking area east of Highway 87 at the entrance to the Tenmile Creek Recreation Path. Walk across the freeway overpass and ascend west from the Mile Marker 195 interchange exit ramp on the Gore Range Trail.

Officers Gulch descends east below Wheeler Lakes

WESTERN WILDERNESS

An amphitheater rises above Gore Creek west of Red Buffalo Pass

Gore Creek

Distance: 14 miles

Elevation Profile: 3,000 feet

Difficulty: Advanced

The Gore Creek Trail ascends east to Red-Buffalo Pass, where it joins the Gore Range Trail west of Silverthorne. The lower mile or two of Gore Creek is a popular destination for waterfall-lovers who can take leisurely walks alongside the tumbling cataracts as Gore Creek drops steeply into the valley. For more ambitious hikers and backpackers, Gore Creek offers dense fir and spruce forest, open wetland meadows, and views of scenic mountain peaks.

The first two miles of trail rise steeply from the trailhead, at 8,700 feet, to a bridge that crosses the stream to the south side, at 9,500 feet. The next two miles of trail pass through wildflowers in wetland meadows broken by stands of fir and spruce.

At four miles, the trail divides with a branch ascending sharply to Gore Lake, on the north side of the valley. The graves of early Swedish settlers Andrew and Daniel Recen mark the junction. Since any log crossing has been washed-out by the heavy snowmelt, there is a traverse through knee-deep water at this point.

At six and a half miles, the trail continues east across Black Gore Creek, a tributary. Again, there is no bridge, but a scattering of rocks and logs provide a crossing a few feet upstream. The trail continues on switchbacks east with views of the boulder fields from which Black Gore Creek arises. The saddle of Red-Buffalo Pass, 11,740 feet, overlooks Red Peak and Buffalo Mountain. The trail continues down to meet the Gore Range Trail, providing access to the South Willow Creek.

How to Get There

Gore Creek Trail provides access to a diverse span of wetland areas along approximately seven miles of pathway that begins at Gore Creek Campground at East Vail. Travel west from Summit County to Exit 180 at East Vail. Proceed under the interstate and head southeast along Bighorn Road for a little over two miles. The trailhead parking area is left of Gore Creek, before the entrance to Gore Creek Campground. Ascend from the registration site and bear right along the trail at the junction with the Deluge Lake Trail.

A reflective pool lies beneath rugged slopes shedding snow to form Gore Creek

Bog orchids bloom in the still waters of the area

Gravesite high up Gore Creek bordered with Arrowleaf Balsamroot

Parry Primrose bloom in early summer beside wetlands

Bistort blooms in open fields high up Gore Creek

Old-Man-of-the-Mountain blooms in high tundra

Lousewort grows in damp, open meadows

Page | 65

Deluge Creek flows toward Gore Creek and Vail

Deluge Lake

Distance: 12 miles

Elevation Profile: 3,200 feet

Difficulty: Advanced

As autumn daylight becomes ever more stunted, the blooms of summer fade in the high country. Shrubs along mountain trails struggle to bear the weight of darkening berries. Bears feast on the bounty in preparation for the long winter fast. Pika and other burrowing animals trim the rock garden flora to add extra lining to their nests as evening temperatures drop toward freezing and clouds darken the sky with threats of the first snowfall. Mosquitoes and biting flies retreat, allowing muffled footfalls to supplant the whining as the only sounds along deep wilderness trails.

Now is the ideal time to climb above the aspen and fir to wish the mountains a peaceful rest through the winter months when the depths of the wilderness become impenetrable. Among the high destinations, the Deluge Lake Trail provides an opportunity to pass by meadows filled with berries and rise to view the last blooms of the season framing the high-country streams.

Beyond the entrance to the Eagles Nest Wilderness Area, false forget-me-nots, mint, mountain chimes, cinquefoil, fireweed, and goldenrod create an orchestra of flowers in the meadows. Rock outcrops along the steep switchbacks of the trail provide views of Vail to the south across the valley.

The Deluge Lake Trail rises quickly from 8,600 feet at the trailhead to 9,210 feet within the first hour. Through dense stands of berries among the aspen, the trail ascends over Gore Creek. Here, serviceberry bushes, *Amelanchier arborea*, provide a bountiful food supply for bears attempting to gain weight before the onset of winter. Mountain gooseberry, *Ribes inerme*, also lines the trail as it winds among the aspen and ancient spruce. Higher, among the dense lodge pole pines, hollygrape, *Mahonia repens*, provides a ground cover of darkening fruits.

Two hours along the trail, at 10,480 feet, wetlands in the dense forest shield yellow arnicas and the pastel blooms of wild geraniums. The trail breaks briefly into open rock sprays, with dramatic drops to the rushing Gore Creek a thousand feet below. Then, the ascent becomes more gradual. After three hours of hiking, 4.5 miles into the hike, the trail gently levels off and follows Deluge Creek up the gulch to the northeast at about 10,800 feet.

The pale royalty of the harebell, *Campanula rotundifolia*, hang like guardians to the trail. Tiny white clusters of the pearly everlasting, *Anaphalis margaritacea*, also brighten the fields along the way. In the wetlands, the star-shaped larkspur, *Delphinium nelsonii*, blooms.

Nearby, the tusks of the little red elephant, *Pedicularis groenlandica*, of the Figwort Family, grow stunted along the brooks.

The Deluge Lake Trail continues across Deluge Creek. As the spruce trees diminish in size among the meadows, large patches of rosy paintbrush, *Castilleja rhexifolia*, mark the path. Views of the rocky amphitheater surrounding Deluge Creek are unimpeded by forest.

After four hours of climbing, the trail reaches a crest 3,172 feet above the trailhead and drops to the lakeshore at 11,690 feet. Drifts of snow on the steep rocky slopes continue to melt into Deluge Lake throughout the summer season. Beside the icy water of the lake, the porcelain blooms of alpine primrose, *Primula parryi*, and stiff red-topped stems of rose crown, *Clementsia rhodantha*, brighten the shore.

How to Get There

The Deluge Lake Trail rises out of East Vail. Driving west from Summit County, take the East Vail turn-off, Exit 180, turning left under the freeway. Proceed east 2.5 miles along Bighorn Road to the trailhead parking area along the west side of Gore Creek. The Deluge Lake Trail breaks away to the left from the Gore Creek Trail at a junction 0.2 miles above the trail register.

Chiming bells line the Deluge Lake Trail

Booth Lake rests below an amphitheater near tree-line at 11,476 feet

Booth Creek

Distance: 12 miles

Elevation Profile: 3,200 feet

Difficulty: Advanced

Whether you are up for a cold-water kayaking experience this spring or a wildflower hunting expedition this summer, Booth Creek Trail may satisfy your desires. Located on the meeting of the granite structure of the Gore Range and the limestone escarpment of the Vail Valley, the Booth Creek Trail offers dramatic rock outcroppings, waterfalls, and an alpine lake along its six-mile length. During the early spring, Booth Creek Trail snow cover is only packed down for the first two hours of climbing to an altitude of approximately 9,500 feet.

Booth Creek Trail offers a great opportunity in the calmer quest for summer wildflowers. The trail climbs among aspen meadows filled with wildflowers along the first mile. Keep a watchful in the dry meadows for the Scarlet Trumpet, *Gilia aggregata*. This distinctive foot-high stem holds brilliant red, five-point trumpets favored by hummingbirds along its stem.

In these grassy meadows, also look for Scarlet Paintbrush, *Castilleja miniata*, meaning colored red. The sturdy spikes hold bracts of double-lobed flowers ranging in color from purple to sunset pink. Paintbrush is hemiparasitic, drawing nutrients from the roots of adjacent plants.

In the darker conifer forest above Booth Falls, look in more shaded areas of fertile soil along the stream banks for dark purple lobes of Monkshood. A poisonous plant, Monkshood sap was used by early hunters to poison arrowheads. *Aconitum dephinifolium*, also known as wolfbane, is a member of the buttercup family.

Among the cool, sheltered rock formations along Booth Creek search for the blooms of Columbine. The Blue Columbine, *Aquilegia caerulea*, is the state flower of Colorado. Columbine is named after the Latin for dove, *columba*, for its delicate winged petals that often hover over pools of water.

Native Americans utilized the ground seeds of the Columbine as an aphrodisiac to charm women. If the Monkshood does not kill you and the Columbine fails to mesmerize you, complete the hike along the shores of Booth Lake, at 11,476 feet, nestled among the steep rocky slopes of Twin Towers and Eyrie Horn in the Gore Range.

How to Get There

Booth Creek Trail ascends six miles and 3,000 feet from East Vail, at 8,400 feet, to Booth Lake, elevation 11,480 feet. Although the trail is arduous at times, the rewards are diverse. Access the trailhead from Summit County by taking the East Vail exit from Interstate 70. Travel west along the north frontage road for about a mile, watching for the Booth Falls Trailhead about two-tenths of a mile north of the freeway.

Booth Falls is a popular destination on Booth Creek

Winter along Booth Creek offers a dramatic perspective on the surrounding cliffs

Piney Lake is surrounded by aspen meadows and wildflowers

Upper Piney Lake

Distance: 14 miles

Elevation Profile: 2,000 feet

Difficulty: Advanced

The features of a great casual hike in the Eagles Nest Wilderness Area may include an alpine lake, frothy waterfalls, wildflowers in season, and a rugged backdrop of mountain peaks. The Upper Piney Trail provides easy access to all of these on a round-trip hike of about eight hours.

Then, hike east to the Upper Piney Lake Trail junction along the north side of Piney Lake, elevation about 9,342 feet. Roaming upstream five miles, Upper Piney Trail gains about 1,000 feet in elevation, making this a fairly easy trek for the Gore Range.

In summer, the aspen meadows along Piney River are filled with the blooms of red columbine, groundsel, lovage, harebell, beardtongue, and wild rose. Foaming waterfalls are a little less than three miles upstream at an elevation increase of only 430 feet. The hike to the waterfall is a casual walk for hikers of almost any age and ability.

Looming eastward above the cataracts are Meridian Peak, Mount Powell, and the Lions Throne. As the trail rises to the south toward Upper Piney Lake, the Kehlstein, 12,005 feet; Twin Towers, 12,692 feet; and Eyrie Horn, 13,041 feet, reveal themselves above the stream.

The hike continues south to Upper Piney Lake, a hike of seven miles, 2,000 feet above the trailhead. Upper Piney Lake is a small lake surrounded by marshes and a dramatic amphitheater.

How to Get There

From Copper Mountain, the Upper Piney Trailhead is a drive of 33 miles. The drive takes a little more than an hour. The first half of the trip is on the I-70 west to Vail Exit 176, west along the frontage road for a mile, then north along Red Sandstone Road for another mile. On the second leg of the journey, take Forest Service Road 700, a gravel road, north for ten miles to the Piney Crossing Trailhead parking area.

Kings crown blooms in wetlands near Upper Piney Lake

Beardtongue penstemon grows in meadows near Piney Lake

Moose are often seen in the wilderness wetlands at dawn and dusk

CONTINENTAL DIVIDE

A nanny and kid mountain goat walk along the Continental Divide

Deer Creek

Distance: 8 miles

Elevation Profile: 2,000 feet

Difficulty: Intermediate

The Deer Creek watershed is created by the snowmelt of the Continental Divide, the eastern boundary of Summit County. Deer creek descends through a valley that once supported several silver mines on Teller Mountain, 12,602 feet. These mines include Lower Radical, Upper Radical, Arabella, Star of the West, Mohawk, and Cashier. The creek flows north in the valley east of Glacier Mountain, 12,443 feet, an area famous for General Teller, Wild Irishman, and Saints John mines.

The Deer Creek Trail begins close to where Deer Creek pours into the Snake River. In an area designated open for multiple uses, the hiking trail is actually an old mining road used for mountain biking, cross-country skiing, and four-wheel-drive recreation. From the trailhead, the hike is four miles from 10,600 feet to the Continental Divide at 12,600 feet. The 2,000-foot vertical ascent on hard-pack road takes about two hours, a typical intermediate Summit County hike.

Since the area is dense with a plethora of deer, elk, moose, ptarmigan, and mountain goats, allowing dogs to be loose is not advisable. However, the Deer Creek area is general National Forest lands where dogs are legally allowed to run. Backcountry camping is allowed. Several established campsites are scattered in the lower valley within a short walk of Deer Creek to filter for drinking water. Local National Forest regulations require dispersed camping be set at least 100 feet from road, trail, or waterway, but established campsites that deviate slightly from the rule are generally acceptable. Campfires are allowed throughout the valley.

Carry standard essentials in a day pack when taking this hike. Due to the exposed high-altitude tundra on the Continental Divide, take either a windbreaker or down jacket on the trip. Carrying two liters of water is not excessive, especially since there is no water source above tree-line, about the last thousand feet of ascent. A high-energy snack, sunglasses, map or GPS, headlamp, pocket knife, adhesive bandages, and cell phone are reasonable supplies. As with any outdoor adventure, pack out any trash and leave-no-trace of your visit.

The Deer Creek Trail rises quickly on switchbacks, past lush fields of wildflowers including primrose, penstemon, Parry primrose, paintbrush, king's crown, and mertensia chiming bells. In the higher tundra, frosty ball thistle and old-man-of-the-mountain grow.

Once on the ridge, hike east along cliffs overlooking Park County, south of the Continental Divide. Walk east to Webster Pass and view the brilliant slopes of Red Cone, 12,801 feet. North, beyond the Snake River and Peru Creek watersheds, the summits of Grays Peak, 14,270 feet, and Torreys Peak, 14,267 feet, should be visible. When the day is quiet, without motorized vehicle traffic and no harassing dogs, I have found ptarmigan among the stunted willow thickets and a herd of mountain goats comprising more than twenty nannies and kids.

A male ptarmigan with orange eyelid watches over his hen above Deer Creek

How to Get There

The drive from Silverthorne to the Deer Creek Trailhead beyond Montezuma is approximately 20 miles. From the I-70 interchange in Silverthorne, drive east to Keystone on Highway 6. At the bridge east of the Keystone Resort parking lot at River Run, exit to Montezuma Road.

Montezuma is a mining town that was settled around 1863 during a major silver boom. Remnants of mining operations from more than a century ago dot the mountain slopes surrounding the community. Beyond the little village are deteriorating roads slicing the sides of the valleys to provide access to the Upper Snake River and Deer Creek, tributary to the westward flowing Snake River. Heading south of Montezuma, Webster Pass Road forks to the east or left, while Deer Creek Road climbs straight south.

Continue straight on a mildly steep and rough road. Drive carefully across water diversion berms and protruding rocks at a slow pace. Proceed to the Forest Service entrance to the Deer Creek watershed. You may park at the large, circular parking area where the Snake River passes beneath the road. Alternatively, you may drive a bit farther up the road and park at the side of the road at an existing pull-out.

The lush Snake River Valley lies below Webster Pass

Webster Pass

Distance: 10 miles

Elevation Profile: 2,300 feet

Difficulty: Intermediate

Webster Pass Road ascends to the sources of the Snake River, streams from the slopes of Sullivan Mountain, 13,134 feet; Landslide Peak, 13,238 feet; Red Cone 12,801 feet; Handcart Peak, 12,518 feet; and Teller Mountain, 12,602 feet; along the Continental Divide. A loop hike beginning at Webster Pass Road and passing northeast through the Snake River watershed to the ridgeline of Teller Mountain involves an intermediate ascent of 2,300 feet across 5 miles, with a total distance of 10 miles and three to four hours of hiking if the loop is completed down Deer Creek Road.

From the parking area south of the intersection with Webster Pass Road, hike north a few tenths of a mile on Montezuma Road and turn east onto Webster Pass Road. After the first mile of hiking, the road exits private lands and passes through a Forest Service gate indicating the start of Forest Service Road 285. The road continues through a beautiful green valley filled with wildflowers growing amid stands of fir and spruce. Willow thickets line the course of the Snake River as it flows south of the road. Among the wetland meadows, white globeflower, blue chiming bell mertensia, red and white paintbrush, white bistort, purple beardtongue, white lousewort, striped mountain clover, blue laurel, yellow cinquefoil, and pink Parry primrose cover the slopes.

The road crosses to the south side of the Snake River about a mile and a half up the valley, at 10,900 feet. In high water, this involves hiking across a boot-high stream in neoprene kayak booties or trampling through the willows to find a combination of boulders and fallen timber on which to balance and jump to stay dry. Once it begins ascending the north face of Teller Mountain, Webster Pass Road gains elevation at a faster rate and becomes impassable for all but the most aggressive high-clearance vehicles.

Three miles into the hike, a junction splits the road. Turning left continues two miles to the top of Webster Pass, 12,100 feet. Instead, begin the steep ascent west on Radical Hill Road, Forest Service Road 286, by turning to the right. Radical Hill Road becomes a broken and narrow path climbing to the abandoned cabin and tailings pile at the Cashier Mine site. The crumbling road continues to the ridgeline of Teller Mountain at about 12,600 feet. Tundra flowers including blue alpine forget-me-not and the stunted yellow sunflower old-man-of-the-mountain clothe the top of Teller Mountain. On a clear day, Grays Peak, 14,270 feet, is visible north beyond the valley of Peru Creek. South of Teller Mountain, the plains of Park County can be seen in the distance.

With 5 miles and the final ascent behind you, proceed west into the Deer Creek watershed. Following Deer Creek Road north will return you to the parking area east of Glacier Mountain and north of Teller Mountain, near the meeting of Deer Creek and the Snake River.

Mining ruins are scattered throughout the area above Montezuma

How to Get There

The drive from Frisco to the Webster Pass Trailhead beyond Montezuma is 20 miles. From Frisco, descend to Silverthorne and take Highway 6 to the east end of Keystone Resort and follow the sign indicating the exit on the right to Montezuma Road. Ascend 5 miles to the Town of Montezuma and proceed 1 mile to the intersection with Webster Pass Road (10,300 feet). Since there is no parking allowed at Webster Pass Road, continue another 0.3 miles to a large circular parking area where the Snake River crosses beneath Montezuma Road.

Kids play on the slopes below Webster Pass on the Continental Divide

Parry clover fills the tundra throughout Colorado

Moonset over the summit of Torreys Peak

Grays and Torreys Peaks

Distance: 8 miles

Elevation Profile: 3,000 feet

Difficulty: Intermediate

Winter is a wonderful season for climbing Fourteeners. White snowfields create a dramatic contrast against the dark rock of windblown ridges. In the willows, white hares and ptarmigan hide. Among the boulders, pikas chirp warnings across the mountain slopes. The calm air creates deceptive warmth under the brilliant sunlight in a crystal blue sky. On the ridges, the temperature plunges below zero under the impact of a snow-blasting breeze. In winter, the hike to the summits of Grays and Torreys constitute a good work-out. From the parking area at Bakerville, the round-trip to reach both summits is more than 14 miles, approximately eleven hours, on a vertical ascent of 4,400 feet,

After the first hour and a half hike on the road up to the trailhead and past mining ruins in Stevens Gulch. From the trailhead, Grays Peak Trail crosses Stevens Creek and continues south through willow thickets at the base of Kelso Mountain, 13,164 feet. After a gradual ascent for a mile and a half to 12,140 feet, a trail sign explains the remaining route to the summit of both peaks. A second crossing of Stevens Creek is the beginning of a steeper ascent through boulders and patches of tundra turf up switchbacks on the eastern slope of Grays Peak. The mild above-freezing warmth of Stevens Gulch is replaced by sub-zero winds at the summit, creating a change in clothing strategy. From Grays, the summits of Mount Bierstadt and Mount Evans are clearly visible southeast of the rounded ridge.

The trail to Torreys Peak descends along a wide saddle, passing a broad cornice of snow clinging to the eastern bowl that must be traversed for the easiest descent. The pointed summit of Torreys is a hike of about an hour from the summit of Grays. Dillon Reservoir and Gore Range can be seen west of Torreys, along with Loveland Pass above Arapahoe Basin. As the setting sun leaves dark shadows across Stevens Gulch, a seven-mile descent remains. Heading down to the saddle and climbing a couple hundred feet toward Grays summit, the trail crosses snowfields and drops down to Stevens Creek to meet the road back to Bakersville.

The switchbacks up to the summit of Grays Peak provide an easy grade for hiking

How to Get There

During the summer, the trailhead to Grays Peak and Torreys Peak can be reached by a low-clearance vehicle, 3 miles above the Bakerville exit on I-70 a few miles east of the Eisenhower-Johnson Tunnels. The Forest Service road is usually maintained for low-clearance vehicles for the 3 miles to 11,300 feet. The summit of Grays is less than 4 miles away at 14,270 feet on a well-maintained trail with easy switchbacks.

Torreys Peak rises from a short saddle north of Grays Peak

Mining ruins remain scattered through the Peru Creek Valley

Argentine Pass

Distance: 5 miles

Elevation Profile: 2,000 feet

Difficulty: Intermediate

Dating back to its beginning as a transportation corridor in 1869, the Argentine Pass Trail is actually the remnant trace of a wagon toll road from Georgetown to mining camps on the western slope of the Continental Divide. Five years earlier, silver deposits were found on the slopes of McClellan Mountain, 13,587 feet, 2 miles north of the area later named Argentine mining district. Argentine Peak, 13,738 feet, was named after the Latin word *argentum*, meaning silver. Ruins of the area mines are plentiful throughout the Peru Creek watershed.

The Argentine Central Railway was constructed on the less-steep eastern face of Mount McClellan from Silver Plume to Waldorf and up to the summit of Mount McClellan. Construction did not begin until 1905, headed by Edward J. Wilcox, owner of 65 mining properties in the Argentine mining district. The rail was extended from Waldorf, a mining town destroyed by an avalanche, to the top of Mount McClellan with the intended destination of Grays Peak, 14,270 feet, as a tourist attraction. The Panic of 1907 brought a collapse of the silver market that ruined the fortune of Wilcox. The railroad was sold at a loss of $256,000 in 1908. The narrow-gauge railway subsequently went bankrupt by 1911. The tracks were removed in 1920.

Argentine Pass Trail is an intermediate trail for Summit County. The distance to the ridge above Horseshoe Basin from the parking pad near the ruins of the Shoe Basin Mine is about 2.6 miles. The elevation gain from 11,300 feet to 13,200 feet offers challenges including scrambles over areas damaged by slides on the steep slopes of Argentine Peak.

Give yourself a few hours to ascend the trail to Argentine Pass. Carry at least a liter of water on a cool day, more if the day is hot. Pack a windbreaker and fleece to prepare for high winds near the ridge.

The path through the Peru Creek Valley is lush with fields of wildflowers. In mid-summer, blue columbine, paintbrush, groundsel, arrowleaf balsamroot, mouse ear, figwort, and penstemon are abundant. In the high alpine stretch of the trail, blue sky pilot, pink moss campion, and yellow old-man-of-the mountain cover the gravel beside the trail.

Moss campion carpets the tundra beside the Argentine Pass Trail

From the top of the pass, Mount Edwards, 13,850 feet rises north along the ridge. West of the pass, Grays Peak, 14,270 feet, forms the west face of Horseshoe Basin, with Ruby Mountain, 13,277 feet, and Cooper Mountain, 12,792, lining the path of the lower Peru Creek Valley to the base of Peru Creek Road.

How to Get There

The Argentine Pass Trailhead is about 16 miles from Silverthorne, east of Keystone. From the I-70 interchange in Silverthorne, drive east on Highway 6 to Keystone and exit to Montezuma Road. Drive 4 miles, crossing a bridge, and take a left turn on Peru Creek Road, Forest Service Road 260. Low-clearance vehicles can reach the junction with Cinnamon Gulch Road, 4 miles up Peru Creek watershed. Either park here for a look at the Pennsylvania Mine Ruins or continue another half-mile to a parking area for Argentine Pass. Hike a bit farther on the road above the ruins of the Shoe Basin Mine to the start of the Argentine Pass Trail.

The East Wall of Arapahoe Basin can be seen from Lenawee Trail

Lenawee Trail

Distance: 7 miles

Elevation Profile: 3,000 feet

Difficulty: Intermediate

The Lenawee Trail offers a glimpse of fall colors as it ascends through groves of young aspen regenerating in the constant upheaval of avalanche flows down the steep slopes of Lenawee Mountain, 13,204 feet. About 1.5 miles up the trail at 11,500 feet of elevation near tree-line, the Lenawee Trail offers expansive views of the area.

From the upper trail, Dillon Reservoir of the Gore Range and the Tenmile Range lie in the distance west of the Snake River Valley. The ridgeline of Lenawee Mountain from 12,550 feet to 13,200 feet overlooks Arapahoe Basin Ski Area and Loveland Pass on the Continental Divide.

Immediately west of Lenawee Mountain is the ridge of Porcupine Peak, 11,803 feet, that forms the wall of Montezuma Bowl. Grizzly Peak, 13,427 feet, forms the north portion of the East Wall beyond the Lenawee Mountain chutes at Arapahoe Basin. Directly north of Lenawee Mountain, Highway 6 ascends on sharp switchbacks to Loveland Pass, 11,980 feet. East of Lenawee Mountain, and out-of-sight unless you climb to the summit, are the Fourteener twins Grays Peak, 14,267 feet, the southern mountain, and Torreys Peak, 14,270 feet, across the saddle to the north.

The Lenawee Trail is a challenging five-hour intermediate hike of 8 miles. The trail has an elevation gain of 2,200 feet from the trailhead at 10,370 feet to Lenawee Mountain ridge at 12,570 feet. Of course, you can split the distance and still enjoy passing through a thicket of young aspen saplings and a rocky overlook 1.5 miles into the hike.

The area is general forest lands, open to a variety of recreation. Wildlife is abundant and includes moose, marmot, coyote, and mule deer. The area is frequented by dog walkers, mountain bikers, dispersed campers, and hunters during the fall season.

The challenging terrain and dramatic changes in the weather of Summit County should be respected. Since a colleague of mine volunteers with the Summit County Search and Rescue group and spends almost every free day of summer on a rescue or recovery mission, I will reiterate the gear that I carry on any day hike.

In cool weather on an intermediate hike through dry forest and tundra that has no natural source of flowing water during most of the year, I carry at least one liter of water. In my pockets, I have adhesive bandages in my wallet, cell phone, Victorinox knife, and a few tissues. In my day pack, I carry a fire starter, two headlamps, extra batteries, fleece, windbreaker, trail snacks such as nuts or cheese, sunglasses, reading glasses, and a global positioning system, regardless of how well I know an area or how far I intend to hike. Even on hikes in the center of cities, I have needed to use my headlamp, adhesive bandages, and my pocket knife.

Loveland Pass and Arapahoe Basin lie north of the Lenawee Trail

How to Get There

The Lenawee Trailhead is about 15 miles from Silverthorne, east of Keystone. From the I-70 interchange in Silverthorne, you will drive east on Highway 6 to Keystone and exit to Montezuma Road. Drive about 5 miles, crossing a bridge over the Snake River, and take a left turn on Peru Creek Road, Forest Service Road 260. Although the gravel road is rough and dips at water diversion berms, low-clearance vehicles can reach the trailhead 2 miles up Peru Creek watershed. The trailhead is clearly marked and small pull-outs offer parking along the south side of Peru Creek Road. The trail ascends the slope north of the road.

The Peru Creek watershed is part of the Argentine mining district, named after the Latin word *argentum*, meaning silver. Beyond the Lenawee Trailhead, you can explore historic mining ruins of the Argentine mining district, including buildings associated with the Pennsylvania Mine and the degraded route of the failed Argentine Central Railway that was constructed beginning in 1905 to serve mining claims owned by Edward J. Wilcox. The Panic of 1907 brought a recession and the collapse of the silver market, bringing a close to the mining in the Argentine area.

A coyote hunts for rodents on a rock outcropping near the Lenawee Trail

TENMILE RANGE

Peak One is a challenging destination on the exposed ridge above Mount Royal

Peak One

Distance: 10 miles

Elevation Profile: 3,800 feet

Difficulty: Advanced

Climbing Mount Royal, 10,502 feet, to reach the summits of Mount Victoria 11,775 feet, and Peak One, 12,933 feet, is a popular and convenient day hike for visitors to Frisco. Although the two-mile hike up Mount Royal is an easy ascent of only 1,300 feet, be forewarned that the trail is on a steep incline over much of this distance. Do not depart from well-established trails. Avoid descending onto the cliffs on the north and west faces of Mount Royal. Many hikers have been rescued from technical routes on the slopes of Mount Royal after being cliffed-out on deceptively easy descents. If early-season snow has fallen, be prepared to wear crampons or micro-spikes to maintain a grip on the slippery inclined plane.

Mount Victoria is a moderately difficult summit to reach with good trail leading to the exposed ridge a few feet above tree-line, only 2,700 vertical feet above the trailhead. The views of the Blue River Valley, Ptarmigan Wilderness, and Eagles Nest Wilderness from the summit are very rewarding compensation for the effort.

The longer, nearly 10-mile round trip hike to the summit of Peak One is a much more strenuous climb of 3,800 feet, with terrain that includes loose rock on very steep slopes. Ascending easy Fourteeners in the area, such as Quandary, Grays, and Torreys Peaks, is safer and less dangerous than attempting to gain the summit Peak One.

From the Peaks Trail parking area at 9,100 feet, head west on an unmarked trail and turn left at the first trail junction to wrap around the east face of Mount Royal. After another fifteen minutes, about a half-mile from the trailhead, bear right and ascend west, crossing two creeks before meeting the Masontown Trail (#9077). Continue west up the Masontown Trail until you find the tailings piles marking the old mining town at the junction with the Mount Royal Trail (#1) at one mile and 9,490 feet.

Masontown was an ill-fated mining community centered on an ore processing mill established in 1866 on the avalanche pathway in the eastern gulch of Mount Royal. By 1872, the site included a boardinghouse, cabins, and milling facilities. A railway reached the base of Mount Royal by 1882, allowing easy transportation of gold and silver ores to Denver. By the turn of the century, Masontown, like most mining operations in Summit County, was a ghost town. In 1912, a deep, unstable snowpack slid off of Mount Royal, burying Masontown. Today, all that remains of Masontown are a few bricks and tailings piles, covered with young aspen trees that rise up quickly after avalanches sweep mountain slopes bare.

Beyond Masontown, follow the straight, steep incline on the Mount Royal Trail west to the junction where the trail divides at 10,250 feet, heading right to the Mount Royal overlook and left to the summit of Mount Victoria. From the top of Mount Royal, excellent access is provided for viewing the south end of the Gore Range. Heading south on the climb to Mount Victoria, the trail passes the remains of a mining cabin with walls still stacked seven logs high.

After three hours of climbing, the trail winds to the top of Mount Victoria, with great views of Buffalo Mountain, Red Peak, and Uneva Peak to the northwest, Peak One to the south, and the Frisco community beside Dillon Reservoir to the northeast.

Buffalo Mountain can be seen north of the Mount Royal Summit

During the descent from the summits, the Mount Royal Trail can be taken from Masontown. Along the way, there is a turn-off to the trail heading east to the Peaks Trail parking area. Alternatively, the Mount Royal Trail continues down to the recreation path, where turning right on the recreation path leads back to the parking circle.

How to Get There

Entering Frisco from I-70 to the west end of Main Street, drive east to Second Avenue. Turn right, heading south, and continue to the intersection with South Cabin Green Trail. Proceed carefully cross the paved non-motorized recreation path and park in the circle beyond "Zach's Place," bench. A connecting trail to the Mount Royal Trail departs west from the parking area, rising to join either of two optional trails that wrap southeast around Mount Royal, 10,502 feet.

Alpine thistle inhabits the tundra above tree-line

Dillon Reservoir covers the Blue River Valley northeast of Mount Victoria

The Miners Creek Trail bisects the valley east of Mount Royal to join the Wheeler Trail

Wheeler Trail

Distance: 14 miles

Elevation Profile: ,000 feet

Difficulty: Intermediate

When he grazed cattle at the base of Copper Mountain around 1880, Judge John S. Wheeler used a trail on the side of the Tenmile Range to get his stock over the mountains before snowfall. Today, that route extends about 14 miles from Copper Mountain to the south end of Summit County at Hoosier Pass. A junction with the Miners Creek Trail on the west face of the Tenmile Range allows passage south, forming a 14.4-mile hike from Copper Mountain to Frisco.

Looking east from Copper Mountain, the summits of Peak Four, 12,866 feet, and Peak Three, 12,676 feet, in the Tenmile Range are the ragged cliffs above Tenmile Creek. Two avalanche chutes merge where the Wheeler Trail begins. One mile south of the trailhead, three other avalanche chutes form the letters "SKY" above the Far East Parking Lot along the east side of Highway 91. The Wheeler Trail turns uphill near the base of the first chute. The trail continues steadily south without a switchback for 3.6 miles from the trailhead.

From the parking area near the exit for Highway 91, hike across the bridge. Turn right to follow Tenmile Creek upstream, one mile south along Highway 91. The trail follows a natural gas pipeline access road to the junction with a bridge crossing Tenmile Creek that replaced an old wooden stock bridge. Across the stream is the Far East Lot, another place to catch the Wheeler Trail. The parking area fills with Copper Mountain Resort visitors in winter.

The junction marks the beginning of the ascent of the Wheeler Trail, at 9,770 feet. The Colorado Trail and Continental Divide Trail share this corridor. Two hours from the trailhead, at 11,215 feet, the Wheeler Trail meets Miners Creek Trail near tree line below Peak Seven, 12,655 feet, and Peak Eight, 12,987 feet.

In order to reach Frisco, hike north along the switchback to cross over the Tenmile Range on the saddle of Peak Six on Miners Creek Trail. Alternatively, proceed to Spruce Creek and Hoosier Pass by continuing on the Wheeler Trail and cross the range on Peak Eight.

The tundra begins at about 11,940 feet, three hours and 4.5 miles from the trailhead. Grouse wander along the trail in the firs. From the open tundra, Copper Mountain Village and the I-70 corridor extend west to Vail Pass in the valley below.

The Miners Creek Trail reaches the summit pass at 12,530 feet, with a total ascent of about 3,000 feet. The crest of the Tenmile Range is 6.2 miles from the trailhead. From the pass, look south to view the Town of Breckenridge.

Descend into the lodgepole pines along the Miners Creek Trail on the east face of the Tenmile Range. The trail crosses Miners Creek twice, affording open views of the cliffs at the crest of Peaks Three and Four.

Six hours into the hike, the Upper Miners Creek Trailhead turns downslope from 10,665 feet. Continue east, crossing Miners Creek again. The trail hooks south briefly around a ridge before crossing another branch of Miners Creek, then follows the creek to a junction with the Peaks Trail. Turn left at the junction with the Peaks Trail for the final 4 miles down the Miners Creek ravine to Frisco.
The trail departs the forest and merges with the pavement of the recreation path through Frisco. Continue north on the paved road to the

trail entrance and bus shelter next to the community center. Catch a Summit Stage bus to the Frisco Station to meet a bus for the return trip to Copper Mountain.

The Tenmile Range south of the saddle across Peak Six

How to Get There

In order to access the Wheeler Trail, drive or ride the Summit Stage to the east entrance of Copper Mountain Village. The trailhead parking area is along the frontage road on the south side of I-70, past the gas station and Copper Mountain Consolidated Metropolitan District Wastewater Reclamation Facility. The parking area is beside Tenmile Creek and the ponds of Wheeler Flats. Cross the stream and turn south toward Freemont Pass.

Lower Mohawk Lake

Mohawk Lakes

Distance: 7 miles

Elevation Profile: 1,400 feet

Difficulty: Beginner

Lower Mohawk Lake is located in the Spruce Creek Trailhead south of Breckenridge. The lake is nestled in a deep amphitheater formed by Pacific Peak, 13,950 feet, and Mount Helen, 13,165 feet, in the Tenmile Range. The hike is an ascent of 1,400 vertical feet, with a total distance of 6.6 miles from the Spruce Creek Trailhead. The elevation of Spruce Creek Trailhead is 10,400 feet, a thousand feet below tree-line.

Mohawk Lakes are near tree-line, surrounded by rocky tundra and krummholz. The Mohawk Lakes Trail provides access to an area with dramatic waterfalls, rich fields of wildflowers, and relics of the mining era.

Allow at least 5 hours to explore the area and plan to descend in early afternoon to avoid the frequent thunderstorms that tend to form over the mountains later in the day. Carry two bottles of water to remain hydrated during the hike or pack a water filter to take water from the stream. Be prepared to find a crowd of hikers on this popular trail, accompanied by many free-roaming dogs.

From the Wheeler Trail junction, the hike to tiny Mayflower Lake is only a mile, with the spectacular spray of Lower Mayflower Falls located near the trail switchbacks a half-mile farther at 11,100 feet. Above the switchbacks are a miner's cabin and the remains of an ore cart tram wheelhouse.

The remains of an ore cart lift, precursor to the modern ski lift

The Pike's Peak Gold Rush of 1858 brought miners to placer gold in the waterways surrounding Denver. However, miners quickly discovered that larger concentrations of precious minerals could be found in the streams of the Central Mountains. The first settlements in the Blue River Valley formed to exploit gold deposits in the Breckenridge area. Within a decade, placer gold recovery declined and hard rock silver mining became more important to the economy of the area.

Silver rose in value due to federal legislation that authorized the United States government to purchase and coin silver under the Bland-Allison Act of 1878. With the increase in the value of ores, mining operations expanded. Federal government purchases of silver nearly doubled under the mandates of the 1890 Sherman Silver Purchase Act. However, the repeal of the Act caused the collapse of the silver market in 1893, leaving many mining camps in ruins.

On the western shore of Lower Mohawk Lake, at 11,860 feet, the walls of one mining cabin remain. A trail leading from the southern shore of Lower Mohawk Lake leads to the Upper Mohawk Lake, 300 feet higher in the gulch.

As you wander among the wetlands, look for alpine wildflower species. You may find artic gentian, inverted bells of white with blue stripes along the sides of its petals. In boggy areas, look for the red elephant figwort, white bog orchid, kings crown, and queens crown. On drier slopes beside the trail, rosy paintbrush and columbine clusters may greet you. Among the rocks, look for alpine forget-me-not, sky pilot, and moss campion. Descend slowly from the lakes and absorb all of the beauty, from gigantic rocky ridges to the tiny blossoms of tundra flowers.

How to Get There

From the Frisco, drive south for 10 miles to the Peak 8 gondola in Breckenridge. Continue for another 3 miles south to Spruce Creek Road, across the highway from the pond called Goose Pasture Tarn. Turn right and ascend west 1.8 miles to Spruce Creek Trailhead. Since the road above the trailhead is not well maintained for low-clearance vehicles, park here. Either continue driving up the road if you have a high-clearance vehicle or hike west for 1.3 miles to the junction with the Wheeler Trail. Hike 0.5 miles down the Wheeler Trail to a large beaver pond where the trail meets the Spruce Creek trail. Turn west on the Spruce Creek Trail to its terminus, then cross the road to find the trail to Mohawk Lakes.

Beaver ponds reflect the Tenmile Range along the lower Spruce Creek Trail

Cabin ruins stand on the idyllic western shore of Lower Mohawk Lake

The amphitheater created by Fletcher Mountain forms the top of Mayflower Gulch

Mayflower Gulch

Distance: 4 miles

Elevation Profile: 1,000 feet

Difficulty: Beginner

Nestled in the magnificent amphitheater below the ragged crest of Fletcher Mountain, 13,951 feet, the ruins of the failed Boston Mining Company gold digs remain among a meadow of wetland wildflowers. Mayflower Gulch is located on the west side of the Tenmile Range. Mayflower Gulch is an accessible and easy trail for summer hiking as well as winter backcountry recreation. The hike involves a gradual ascent of 2 miles from 10,990 feet to 12,000 feet on an old mining road. Providing time for exploration and photographs, the hike can be completed within two hours.

Wildflowers are abundant in the wetlands on the north side of the road, bordering Mayflower Creek. Globeflower, elephant tusk, cinquefoil, lousewort, alpine smelowskia, bistort, paintbrush, chiming bells, columbine, arnica, beardtongue, alpine clover, and mountain goldenrod grow thick in the fertile fields of the valley.

After ascending for an hour, passing the fallen remains of a cabin and an ore loading chute, the trail breaks out of the forest and reveals the remnant structures of a mine boarding house and settler's cabin on the left side of the road. The road branches south and ascends Gold Hill if you want to continue farther. On the tundra ridge of Gold Hill there are many more signs of early mining attempts on the pocketed slopes rising to the rocky ridge at 12,400 feet.

From the top of Gold Hill, you can see the Clinton Creek watershed. The stream descends northwest from the steep wall of Wheeler Mountain, 13,900 feet, and Clinton Peak, 13,857 feet, on the Continental Divide, forming Clinton Reservoir in the valley below. West of Clinton Reservoir lies the site of the Kokomo mining settlement, south of Jacque Peak, 13,205 feet, and Tucker Mountain, 12,421 feet.

Kokomo was the center of population growth in the valley of Tenmile Creek, just below Gold Hill, beginning with silver discoveries in 1878. The area population swelled to a high estimated at 10,000 miners during the following three years. In 1881, Kokomo was leveled by fire. Although cabins were rebuilt, the silver deposits quickly diminished in value and the area sustained only a few hundred people past the turn of the century. The Climax Mine purchased most of the land throughout the Upper Tenmile valley to serve as a tailings deposit site for the open-pit operation near the top of Freemont Pass.

How to Get There

Drive west from Frisco for 7 miles to the Copper Mountain exit from the I-70. Head south for 6 miles, ascending on Highway 91 to the Mayflower Gulch parking pad on the east side of the highway. Tailings ponds of the Climax Mine fill the valley west of the highway. If you reach Clinton Reservoir on the left side of the highway, you have gone 2 miles too far.

A yellow-bellied marmot chirps a warning and stands at his burrow entrance

The trail up the eastern face of Quandary reveals a false summit

Quandary Peak

Distance: 7 miles

Elevation Profile: 3,500 feet

Difficulty: Intermediate

Quandary Peak, 14,265 feet, is a popular beginner Fourteener due to its easy access and established hiking path. Quandary is probably among the most often attempted and least attained summits among the highest peaks in Colorado. Since it attracts many novices, I have seen most hikers turn back after two miles of hiking up to tree-line at about 12,000 feet.

One winter weekend, I began hiking from the trailhead at dawn, surrounded by twenty hikers. By the time I reached the summit, only two other hikers were on the mountain. Counter-intuitively, the three hikers who reached the summit were middle-aged, while all of the young hikers in their twenties had quit below 13,000 feet. On Fourteeners, slow and steady persistence often wins the race.

On this warm fall day, I began my ascent after noon and immediately met two young, disoriented hikers visiting from east of the Continental Divide. I led them north along the Forest Service access road a short distance and followed the Quandary Trail northwest into the forest.

While I carried two ice-cold liters of water on my pack and paused frequently to sip, I did not observe them drinking any fluids. I allowed them to set the pace, two miles an hour for 1,000 vertical feet to 12,200 feet, reaching the krummholz and tundra. Despite the ideal climbing conditions, they were done. I suspect that they were dehydrated, unconditioned to long-term activity, and suffering from an anaerobic accumulation of lactic acid in their muscles. When they mentioned using a stair-stepper in a gym, I explained that they would probably need to complete 7,000 steps to attain the mile of vertical that is typical to the summit of a Fourteener.

I continued following the trail west on the ridge, enjoying the view of Hoosier Pass, the Upper Blue River Valley east of Quandary, and Grays Peak, 14,270 feet, and Torreys Peak, 14,267 feet, at the distant horizon. Climbing through the rock fields and tundra at 12,700 feet, I met a group of mountain goats grazing on the brown turf scattered among the rocks. A couple of kids huddled closely to the sides of their nannies, while an odd one out bleated to call its mother near. I had passed a hunter carting out a goat on my way up the mountain and feared that the solitary kid was now an orphan, victim of a killer in search of an easy trophy.

Proceeding past the first false summit at about 13,000 feet, my pace dropped below one mile an hour. Over the top of North Star Mountain, the section of the Continental Divide separating Summit and Park counties, I could see other Fourteeners south of Quandary.

A nanny and her kid stand above the cliffs on the south face of Quandary Peak

The easy summits of Democrat, 14,148 feet; Cameron, 14,238 feet; Lincoln, 14,286 feet; and Bross, 14,172 feet, are usually approached from Kite Lake, west of Alma. After 3.7 miles of ascending along the rock-strewn rib of Quandary, I reached the summit. The steep cliffs of the western slope were below me. I could see Buffalo Mountain and the Gore Range spread across the horizon to the north. Holy Cross Ridge formed the western horizon. The sharp, ragged ridge of Fletcher Mountain formed the wall immediately west of Quandary, blocking a view of Mayflower Gulch and Clinton Reservoir.

On the summit of Quandary Peak, the view south includes Bross, Lincoln, and Democrat

As the sun dipped low in the sky, I ate a handful of nuts, drank from the bottom half of my second liter of water, and began descending to the base of Quandary. At about 13,000 feet, the lonely kid began following me. He attempted to join another kid, but instead of comfort was met with a head butt from the horns of the nanny. For a mile, the solitary kid trotted beside me, bleating for his mother. Casting a melancholy mood, I knew this kid would be the first of his cohorts to succumb from exposure when snow covered the mountain and he was unable to share the warm companionship of his nanny.

A male ptarmigan is almost invisible on Quandary Peak in winter

How to Get There

The Quandary Trailhead, east and south of the Ten Mile Range, is 8 miles south of Breckenridge on Highway 9. After passing Goose Pasture tarn on the east side of the highway, continue through the Town of Blue River to the switchbacks that lead up to Hoosier Pass. Turn right on Blue Lakes Road and bear right to the Quandary Trailhead parking area. The trail ascends gently through the forest on the east face of Quandary Peak.

Featured Wildflowers

Cornhusk lily	6
Aspen aster	7
Fireweed	7
One-sided penstemon	8
Larkspur	8
Green gentian	14
Globeflower	15
Marsh marigold	15
Blue columbine	18
Arnica	19
Wild iris	19
Scarlet gilia	20
Peavine	20
Rosy paintbrush	24
Mountain gentian	41
Mariposa lily	43
Monkshood	44
Elephant tusk	44
Avalanche lily	51
Calypso orchid	54
Bog orchid	62

Arrowleaf balsamroot	63
Parry primrose	64
Bistort	64
Old-man-of-the-mountain	65
Lousewort	65
Chiming bells	68
Kings crown	73
Beardtongue	74
Parry clover	81
Moss campion	87
Alpine thistle	95

Pika harvest tundra flowers and store them among the boulders for winter

Kim Fenske has been hiking Colorado wilderness areas for many years. He served as a wilderness ranger and on the board of directors of Friends of the Eagles Nest Wilderness and Sierra Club. He has been an outdoor recreation columnist for the Copper Cable; Summit County Citizens Voice; and Summit Daily News. Furthermore, he has published hiking guides: *Fourteeners for the Rest of Us*; and *Hiking Colorado: Holy Cross Wilderness*.

Made in the USA
Monee, IL
21 November 2024

70800937R00069